Praise for Excellence for Influence

"Work is not the result of the fall of man but was divinely sanctioned by God from the beginning when he placed Adam in the garden to be a gardener. From that first tending of the garden, Adam learned what it was to work excellently and how such work reflected the glory of God. Modern believers have lost that sense of glorious purpose, choosing instead worldly success as the plumbline to measure their purpose in this world. In *Excellence for Influence*, Jonah Erbe defines work using Scripture as the guide, not modern standards of achievement. Striving for biblical excellence in everything our hands are set upon to achieve creates an inevitable sense of purpose for which we were created. This work reminds us that work and influence are two specific areas in which all believers are to glorify and reflect the glory of God."

— Dustin Benge, Provost and Professor of Preaching at Union School of Theology, Bridgend, Wales, and Oxford, England.

"Take a seat, grab a coffee, and get ready to learn. Through authenticity and vulnerability Jonah works through what it looks like to walk out a faithful life to Christ in your career. Don't miss out on this book!"

– Garrett Kahrs, Author of "Labeled" and "#Relationshipgoals," Director of Encounter Young Adults & President of Dealing Hope

"It's a privilege to work. Our friend, Jonah, is on to something in his latest book – *Excellence for Influence*. He does a remarkable job of challenging us to know we are God's crowning work of creation, shaped for meaning and purpose, as we live out our vocation to give a correct opinion of God to others."

– Dr. Byron and Carla Weathersbee, Co-Founders and Executive Directors, Legacy Family Ministries

"Jonah has a desire to glorify God in the workplace with the talents he has been given. He wants to steward well! This book will motivate you to do the same, or ask yourself, 'Why am I not doing this?'"

– Norris Blount, President/CEO of Excelsior Staffing

"*Excellence for Influence* is a refreshing reminder that all of our earthly pursuits should glorify our Creator. As I read the book, it helped me refocus on a Kingdom mindset approach to influence and work place excellence. It brought back the heaviness and weight of our biblical calling to influence those around us with our actions and words towards nothing other than Christ. Like all things worldly, we have seen the definition of influence shift towards persuasion for all things self-gratification, but that isn't the call on our lives. Through biblical examples, Jonah points us to pursue excellence through the sanctification process of embracing failure and hardship while embracing Jesus' never-ending grace. He encourages us to get outside of our "comfortable Christianity," to commit to hard work, and to faithfully pursue excellence with all of our God-given talents. This book is a must-read for followers of Christ to re-center our attention to the influence we have been given and to steward it well."

> – Tara Austin, Founder and Owner of Shop Ruthie Grace

Excellence for Influence

Excellence for Influence:

The Importance of Pursuing Christ-Centered Faithfulness in Your Career

By Jonah Erbe

Foreword by Jonathan Pokluda

Copyright © 2021 Jonah Erbe

All rights reserved.

ISBN-13: 9798458396585

This book is dedicated to my incredible wife, Brooke. You are the embodiment of faithful, Christ-centered excellence in all areas of life in the way you serve others, love your family, and point others to Jesus. Thank you for your love, encouragement, and your companionship. You are my best friend and a constant reminder of God's grace in my life. I love you.

Please share what God is teaching you, what ideas you have taken away from this book, any impactful quotes, and more by using ***#ExcellenceForInfluence*** on all forms of social media.

Table of Contents

Acknowledgements 1

Foreword by Jonathan Pokluda 3

Introduction 7

Chapter One: Common Misconceptions 22

Chapter Two: What Does the Bible Say About Excellence? 41

Chapter Three: Examples of Excellence 52

Chapter Four: Modeled for You and Me 73

Chapter Five: Wasting Time 83

Chapter Six: Whatever You Do 92

Chapter Seven: The Balance Between Excellence & Perfection 104

Chapter Eight: Faith Over Fear 125

Chapter Nine: Who Could Be Against Us? 140

Chapter Ten: Multiplication of Impact 153

Chapter Eleven: Kingdom Growth 168

Chapter Twelve: What if? 182

Conclusion 196

Contact Information 205

Sources by Chapter 207

Acknowledgements

Thank you to so many of you who helped me on this endeavor. This would not be possible without you.

A few specific individuals I would like to recognize:

Jonathan Pokluda: Thank you for agreeing to write the foreword to this book. You are an amazing leader who stewards your gifts and talents faithfully well. Thank you for pastoring our church, Harris Creek. Thank you for loving others well. Thank you for being a constant reminder of what Christ-centered excellence looks like. Thank you for using your influence to point others to Jesus. I am honored to call you a friend and brother in Christ.

Dr. Clay Butler: Thank you for professionally editing this book. You took my ideas and original writings and actually made them legible. That is quite the accomplishment! Thank you for using your gifts and influence to glorify the Lord. I am so grateful to know you and learn from you.

Dustin Benge, Norris Blount, Garrett Kahrs, Dr. Byron and Carla Weathersbee, and Tara Austin: Thank you all for your incredible recommendations for this book project. Thank you for taking time out of your busy schedules to read this work and attach your names to it. I admire all of you and am grateful to call you brothers and sisters in Christ.

Original Readers: You know who you are. From family members, to my life group, to friends, to colleagues, and more, thank you for reading the initial rough draft of this project and providing thoughts and insights. Your wisdom provided immense clarity for me. It is such a joy to know and pursue the Lord alongside all of you.

Foreword by Jonathan Pokluda

I first met Jonah on twitter. There is plenty of critical tweets out there, so when there is a consistent source of encouragement, I noticed. Our family moved to Waco, TX to lead a church that Jonah attended. After every message Jonah had a take away, a word of encouragement, and something he wanted to share with his followers. When he asked to meet, I said ok. When he told me he wanted to write a book, I sensed I was supposed to help. After all, it's not often you meet someone with such worldly gifts so focused on the Kingdom. I think we have something to learn from Jonah.

You might be familiar with the quote attributed to St. Francis of Assisi, "preach the gospel at all times, when necessary, use words." Though it does present a good sentiment about our actions being Christ-like, to share the gospel, we must use words. After all the gospel is a story.

Romans 10:14 says, "*How, then, can they call on the one they have not believed in? And how can they believe in the one of whom they have not heard? And how can they hear without someone preaching to them?"*

In fact, if St. Francis were here today, I think that *he* would agree that words are necessary. There are a couple of things to note about St. Francis that could help explain what he meant.

We should be sharing the gospel everywhere we go and especially where we're placed. Jonah gets this. He has a passion for people to use their professional calling to bring people to know Jesus. In Matthew 5 Jesus calls us to be the light of the world. The Light of The World calls you and I to push back darkness in this world. In the first century lights were expensive. In the 21st century lights are still very expensive. I remember when Monica and I built a house, we blew the budget on light fixtures. I tried to cut some back, but our builder said our house would be too dark. After trying to convince my wife that we could get brighter bulbs and more mirrors, I caved and had to pay up for more light fixtures. When our house was finished, I remember the builder coming by and looking carefully at some pendants that hung over the island in our kitchen. "Those are off by about six inches. They'll have to be moved," he said. The ceiling was already finished out with texture and paint. "It's fine I said. I can't even notice." "No." He replied, "where you put lights is very important." He's a good builder. So, is God. God has carefully hung lights all over your city. He's placed you in a cube farm, a corner office, or behind a cash register somewhere. Or maybe you're in a classroom. Wherever you are, you're somewhere I'm not and somewhere Jonah is not. So, I know his passion is to call you to be a light there. God has placed you there on purpose.

When I worked at AT&T, I was on the 8th floor of a high rise we called, "building four." Every morning I would walk through two security checkpoints to get up there. I had a name badge that I'd show to the first security guard and then I'd have to swipe it at the second check point. Everyone on my floor had a similar badge. I worked in a cubical, surrounded by eight close neighbors. We saw each other every day. On some days we'd go to lunch together. On other days we'd do happy hour. I look back on my time there with great regret. I wish I would have been bolder in sharing my faith. I may never see those people again, and today I cannot get to the eighth floor of building four at AT&T. I no longer have my security badge. I could get into Afghanistan armed with the Gospel easier than I could the eighth floor of building four.

Likewise, you will go somewhere this week that I cannot visit. Maybe it's behind the counter at the bank or coffee shop you work at. If I go back there, I will get some funny looks at minimum, or maybe get arrested. God, however, has placed you there. To be a light. I've been to the jungles of Africa, the jungles of The Amazon, and the mountains of Haiti, but Corporate America is the darkest mission field I've ever seen.

That's why Jonah wrote this book. He wants you to know that you have been called to push back darkness where God has purposely placed you.

Introduction

Can we agree on something? The word "influence" has taken on a new meaning in the last decade. When we hear that word, we now tend to think of social media advertisements and red carpets. However, I would like to make the argument that there are only two types of people: Those who make an impact on the lives of those around them, or influencers, and those who do not. For better or worse, certain people have had the ability to capture the hearts of millions to start a movement, a company, an industry, or a revolution. There have been people of every generation who have separated themselves as true influencers.

When someone says "influencer," who comes to mind? A few names in the world of business that immediately strike me are men and women like Warren Buffett, Sara Blakely, Steve Jobs, Barbara Corcoran, Bill Gates, Mark Zuckerberg, and Jeff Bezos. Whether you agree or disagree with any of them on their beliefs, morals, or politics, we can all agree that they have one thing in common: They have taken God-given gifts and used them to become some of our generation's top influencers in the world of business. The businesses these people run have trickled down and affected all of our lives in the process. We have all felt the effects of their excellence and influence.

What makes these people excellent? There have been many studies conducted attempting to solve that very question. However, none of the studies can come to a direct correlation between each of their successes. They all have such different stories. Some were born poor; some were born rich. Some went to college; some never finished middle school. Some thought outside of the box and possessed immense creativity; some were direct and to the point. The list goes on and on. The only takeaway to be seen is that every single story seems to be different. Sure, there may be some similarities in some stories (To make it onto the cover of Forbes, the main requirement seems to be that you absolutely must start a company in your garage). If all of these stories are different and there are no correlations to be drawn, then what is the purpose of mentioning all of these people in the same chapter or even trying to analyze them all together? I believe that there is a glimmering similarity. As cliché as it may sound, it cannot be found in a statistic or a study. There is one factor that separates the influencers from the rest, and it is this: for better or worse, they were faithful every day to use their God-given abilities to pursue excellence.

They never gave up. They persevered through trials. They invested time into their strengths and stayed away from their weaknesses. They decided to be excellent.

When Steve Jobs was fired from Apple, he stayed the course. He became so valuable to the entire industry that Apple had no choice but to hire him back. He then not only revolutionized computers, but he created entire new industries. One man went from being fired to changing the lives of nearly every single person. Apple is now worth over $1 trillion.

If you want to see an inspiring picture, Google "Jeff Bezos' First Office."[1] In that picture you will see Bezos sitting at a desk you could most likely purchase for under fifty dollars, in a tiny office with grayish walls, at night, staring into an old computer. There is hardly anything hanging on the walls. The one piece clearly hanging up on the wall is a crooked white banner with the words "amazon.com" spray painted in blue on it. Fast forward from that picture in 1999 to now, and Bezos is the first person ever to have a net worth of over $200 billion[2], and Amazon is worth over $1.7 trillion.[3]

Before you close this book because you are thinking "I've heard these stories before. I know they are worth billions of dollars, but what about me?" Stick with me. Yes, these men and women have earned large amounts of money, achieved great things, and have changed the world.

But how does this apply to us? Whether you are a CEO, a leader trying to bring your company to an IPO, an employee working to get that next promotion, a currently uninspired associate attempting to find a new job, a teacher, a pastor, a full-time parent, or simply an individual trying to pay your rent for the next month, this book is for you. These influencers achieved worldly success in many ways, and there are many lessons to be learned from their stories. However, there is much more to being an influencer than making money and owning a massive company.

The kind of influence we are talking about has nothing to do with net worth, checkmarks next to your name on social media, or prestigious awards and titles. The influence we will be discussing throughout this entire book is the only kind that matters: the ability to point people to Jesus through the Gospel wherever you are, using your God-given gifts, at all times. Like it says in Esther 4:14, you have come to your position for such a time as this. Sure, when we are excellent, money and fame may follow, but those are not guaranteed and should never be the goal. In fact, what is guaranteed in

Scripture is that when we follow Jesus, there will be suffering. In case you don't believe me, check out 2 Timothy 3:12, 2 Corinthians 4:17, Romans 8:18, 1 Peter 5:10, or just read through the lives of the 12 Disciples. This Biblical influence may have its moments of worldly success, but it will also be filled with worldly struggles. However, if you are willing to take the challenge to become Biblically Excellent for Gospel-Centered Influence, I can guarantee you that it will be worth it.

In Matthew 28:19 we are called to, "Go and make disciples of all nations, baptizing them in the name of the Father and of the Son and of the Holy Spirit." We are all called to be influencers. The final calling left to us by Jesus is to basically go be an influencer for the Kingdom of God.

Are you doing this? No, I am not asking if you go on mission trips, go to church, and attend Bible studies. These are fantastic things, but that is not what I am asking. What I am asking is this: Are you using the gifts God has given you to go and make a difference in the circles that God has specifically placed you? Does everyone in your circles know the Gospel of Jesus? Does everyone in your circles even know you follow Jesus? To sum up this question and to bring it into the focus of the entire book: Are you pursuing excellence to gain influence to spread the Gospel to more people?

In this world, to have influence, you must be excellent. Notice I did not say you have to be rich or become a CEO. All I said was you have to be excellent. God has given you a certain set of skills and talents. Are you using them to their fullest extent? Are you known in your office as the hardest worker? Are you serving others every single day even when it brings you no immediate benefits? Are you going to bed exhausted every night from the amount of work you put in physically, mentally, spiritually, professionally, and relationally that day? Tragically, most of the world is not doing this on a consistent basis. In the words of Pastor Earl McLellan of Shoreline City Church, "Favor follows hustle."[4] Before the fall of man, God called us to work. Work was not a punishment, but a perfect gift in the Garden of Eden. When man stopped working and became lazy, he gave the enemy the chance to creep in and start spewing lies. If favor and influence follow hustle, then I think it is safe to assume that sin and ineffectiveness follow laziness.

There is a saying my grandfather used to always say, "Idle hands are the devil's workshop." You may have heard something like this quote before. When I was younger, I thought this was just a corny saying. However, I now realize that it holds a lot of truth. There have been studies that have come out in the last couple of decades that show the less you work, the more likely you are to commit a crime. I, nor those who have done the studies, are saying that those who are unemployed are bad or that they are surely destined to do bad things. However, it does say that when we are not working, there is a higher likelihood that we will do things we should not be doing.

I think back to when I was a kid on summer break. During the school year I was incredibly busy with school, homework, sports, and other activities. During the summer, however, I had much more free time on my hands. I think back to how my friends and I spent our free time, and I cannot help but agree with those statistics. While we were not breaking the law, we were definitely far from productive and had a tendency to be lazy. I venture you would say the same about yourself and those you know as well.

During the Covid-19 pandemic of 2020, there was one thing that was for sure: many of us had more time than usual. What happened during that time? Violent crimes increased, suicide went up, domestic violence went up, addictions increased, bad habits were formed, and if we are being honest, we can probably all agree our waistlines may have increased a bit too.[5] During the first few weeks of the pandemic, some boasted in these grand plans of how they were going to read through the Bible, workout like never before, clean up their homes, get caught up on work, learn to cook healthy and many other large claims. After about two or three weeks, however, most of these goals were completely thrown away and laziness kicked in. This laziness is simply part of our fallen and sinful human condition. It is our natural tendency. To be excellent, we must daily surrender our natural tendencies at the foot of the cross of Christ. Only through daily surrender and constant provision from the Lord can we begin to override and replace our sinful tendencies with holy ones.

If we take our own personal experiences and the statistical evidence that is available, it all supports the idea that God created work for our good, not as a punishment. Therefore, since we can agree that work is created for our good by a perfect God, we should also realize that the more we do our work as unto the Lord, and the better the quality of our work output, the more we are following what God has called us to. The work we do every day, and the calling God has placed on all of humanity are not separated, but actually completely intertwined. If we are executing our work for the glory of the Lord and applying maximum effort to our various roles in life as unto the Lord, then influence will follow. Excellence brings influence. People flock to those who are excellent at what they do. Combine excellence in what you do with the calling from Christ to make disciples and think of how many people could be impacted for the Kingdom.

There are leaders and influencers who are excellent at what they do, but they do not know Jesus. However, these people are changing the world. They may not be attempting to further the Kingdom of God, but they are making an impact on the entire globe. Some of these influencers are doing what we would consider to be "good things." They are helping the poor and needy, opening schools, opening hospitals, providing jobs, giving money to charities, and much more. While these men and women are meeting many physical needs, they are not providing insight into the only thing that can fill the God-shaped hole that fills the heart of every man, woman, and child. The world doesn't need another solution or strategy, the world needs Jesus. We have the opportunity to take Jesus to the world in our workplaces and through our careers. Where the previously discussed influencers are only meeting physical needs, you have the opportunity to take generosity and influence a step further and point others to the cure for all eternal needs: the Gospel message. Every ounce of our lives should point others to Jesus, even when we are working.

"I like your Christ, I do not like your Christians. Your Christians are so unlike your Christ." If you are like me, this is probably not the first time you have heard or read this quote from Mahatma Gandhi. This quote should break our hearts! Does the way we as the body of Christ present ourselves at your office and in our profession look like Christ? Are we continuously striving to outdo others with our acts of service? Are we the most respectful people to our bosses and our clients? Do we shut down any and all office gossip in the pursuit of unity? Are we the first to take on that extra project that doesn't fall into our job description solely to help others? Are we peacemakers? Are we individuals worth looking up to? Are we actively trying to gain influence in our workplaces and in the circles the Lord has placed us to proclaim the Gospel of Jesus Christ, or are we okay with working just hard enough to get by, get home, and get a paycheck?

We have been given the gift of the Holy Spirit. Jesus lives in each and every one of us who has professed our faith and trust in Him. We have the same power that raised Lazarus from the dead living inside of us, and the same power that resurrected Jesus Christ (Romans 8:11). Imagine if we as

Believers applied that kind of confidence only found in the cross of Christ into our work environments. Imagine if a new wave of Christians rose up and became excellent workers. Imagine if Christians became leaders in companies and communities all over the world. What if the men and women that possessed large amounts of influence in the world pointed all of the glory and honor back to Jesus and served like Jesus? How much different would the world look? How many more people would hear the Good News? These are the questions I want you to consider throughout this book.

I have one last thought before we move on to the next chapter. Maybe this is coming across as a little too bold to you. Many may think it is completely foolish to dream of a world like this. However, throughout this book, I ask that you carry the words of Ephesians 3:20-21 with you. It says, "Now to him who is able to do far more abundantly than all that we ask or think, according to the power at work within us, to him be glory in the church and in Christ Jesus throughout all generations, forever and ever. Amen." We serve a God that is able to do far more abundantly than we could ask or imagine. Let's dream big and keep Him at the forefront of our ambitions. Will you join me on this journey?

Part One: What Is Excellence?

Chapter One

Common Misconceptions

We must first put aside some common misconceptions of what excellence is not before we can openly discuss what excellence truly is. The world is full of noise. Between social media, texts, online videos, streaming services, seminars, books, television shows, blogs, podcasts, radio shows, politics, and more, it is becoming increasingly more difficult to block out noise. In 2020, people saw on average anywhere from 6,000 to 10,000 ads in one day alone![1] However, to think for ourselves, at some point we must block out all of the sounds crying out for our attention to develop our own opinions of what is true and what is not. This is something we must do for excellence.

Before we move any further in this journey together, I think it is of utmost importance to clarify that we cannot do anything listed in this book if we have not first put our faith in the grace, death, and resurrection of Jesus. If you have already done so, and you are completely sure that your soul belongs to Jesus, then feel free to skip this paragraph. However, if you are not 100% sure, then let's take a moment to make the most important decision you could ever make. God loved you so much that He sent His one and only Son, Jesus, to die a brutal, tortuous death on a murderous weapon of violence, the cross (John 3:16). We have all sinned and therefore are unworthy to be in the presence of the Lord and Creator of the universe (Romans 3:23). Since we have all sinned, that would identify us all as sinners. The payment required of those who are sinners is nothing short of death and eternal punishment and torment in hell away from God. However, because of the free gift given to us in the death and resurrection of Jesus, we can now have eternal life with God

(Romans 6:23). God loves you, and He sent His Son to die for you. Jesus died and rose to life after being buried in a tomb for three days. He then ascended into heaven where He is right now sitting next to our Lord and Savior. He is alive. He is real. He loves you. You don't have to be identified as a sinner anymore. You can be identified as forgiven by Jesus. Don't let another moment pass without giving your life to Him. If you want to give your life and eternity to God, confess to God that you are a sinner, ask Him to forgive you of those sins, declare that you are putting your faith and all of your hope in the death and resurrection of Jesus, and that you now want to live for Him in all you do. Once you have done this, you are saved for all of eternity. There is nothing, no past sin, no current sin, and no future sin, that can snatch you out of the palm of God's loving hands (John 10:28). Welcome to the family of Believers. Please begin attending a local, Bible-believing church, and find other Christians who can encourage you and walk through life with you. Most of all, welcome to the Family. I can't wait to see you in heaven one day. You have taken the first and most important step you could possibly take. Biblical excellence starts with putting your trust and faith in the death and resurrection of Jesus. Biblical community after accepting Christ is absolutely vital as you navigate life as a new creation. If you don't know how or where to go to find a Biblical community, please see my personal contact information at the back of this book and send me an email or reach out on social media. I will do whatever I need to do to find a local, Bible-believing church that you can start attending and help you get in touch with someone there.

Now that you have taken that first step, let's get to work and tackle some other misconceptions that are widely accepted.

The first lie I want to tackle up front is the belief that excellence equals wealth. That is simply not the case and not what we are discussing in this book. Yes, sometimes excellence brings forth wealth, and that is not a bad thing. However, you could be an excellent full-time parent and not become the next Arianna Huffington in regards to wealth. You could be the best mom or dad in the history of the world and raise your children exceptionally well, which is incredibly valuable! Some of the most influential people in the entire world are people that the majority of civilization has never heard of. Think of the hardest workers in your community that run non-profits, take in foster children, or simply work hard and excellently at a lower-paying job. They may not make a lot of money, but simply earn enough to provide for their families. However, they are working incredibly hard with the gifts God has given them, and are influencing many people throughout their career.

We are looking for Biblical excellence, not worldly wealth. So, as we continue our journey through discovering and improving on our own excellence, please do not hold the thought in the back of your mind that your pay stub must increase or you are not doing well. That the amount of your pay stub is indicative of the measure of your Biblical influence is 100%, categorically false.

In reality, some of the most excellent, influential, and faithful people you have ever met are probably the opposite of wealthy and famous. There are faithful parents, faithful teachers, faithful front-line workers, and many more who simply do their work with excellence to the glory of the Lord, share the Gospel with those around them, and make an eternal impact. In this book we will be discussing and using examples of famous business leaders, but please know that all of these principles do not just apply to those in the world of business, but to every other area of life as well. God calls us to be excellent everywhere, not just at the office. The goal is to use whatever influence we have through our career of choice to point others to the Gospel and grow that influential possibility through excellence so we can reach even more people.

Another misconception that I think needs to be thrown out immediately is what the world says excellence looks like. Let's be honest, if you open social media right now, what will you see? Most likely you will see someone doing something you wish you were doing. Little do you know that the person who just posted their amazing beach resort picture is actually struggling immensely with depression, anxiety, debt, relationship issues, job-loss, declining health conditions, or potentially an uncountable number of other obstacles the world can bring. Let's not fall into the trap that excellence looks like a fake representation of our lives through a screen. In fact, an article put out by HealthLine actually points out the ever-increasing list of negative physical and mental health issues social media and screens can cause. According to the study, about 77% of Americans have at least one social media profile.[2] The article goes on to declare that studies show social media increases negative functions such as "depression, anxiety, sleep-disorders, lower self-esteem, inattention, and hyperactivity."

I use social media. I enjoy social media. There is a huge amount of benefits that social media can bring. However, as we sinful humans tend to do, we ruin it. Think about anything that is good, and you can probably find a way we sinners have been able to mess it up. For the remainder of this book, do not allow thoughts of fake excellence brought on by social media and technology into your mind. Block those false ideals out starting now.

Another lie that I want to tackle up-front is that excellence is not a necessity. Society has shown time and time again that mediocrity is okay, but excellence is better. The world says if you want to be mediocre, that is perfectly fine and normal. If you want to be excellent then that is good too, but don't push your standards on someone else. This is a complete and utter falsehood for us who know Jesus.

There is no place in Scripture where Jesus says to do the minimum amount of work in any area of life and that it will be acceptable. In fact, Scripture says quite the opposite in 2 Corinthians 8:7. It says, "But as you excel in everything - in faith, in speech, in knowledge, in all earnestness, and in our love for you - see that you excel in this act of grace also." The Bible calls us to excel in every single thing in which we partake. From the smallest email to the largest presentation at a world-conference, be excellent. Laziness has no place in the Kingdom of God. Where the world says excellence is optional, the Bible says excellence is the standard.

God calls us to be excellent time and time again in Scripture. This means that no matter what our department goals may be, what our boss' goals for us are, or what the world's standards for us are, we are held accountable to a much higher authority: the Creator of the universe. What does the Creator ask of you? Your best, every single time. Notice God doesn't ask us for someone else's best, but YOUR best. This is another major misconception I want to tackle in this chapter.

I think the largest misconception that humanity and society deal with today is the lie of comparison. Theodore Roosevelt said, "Comparison is the thief of joy." Almost all negativity and sin are derived from a place of comparison to someone or something else. Before we continue with this book, we absolutely must put to death the idea that comparison has any place within the realm of Biblical excellence. Let me give a personal example to help explain this.

I love sports. If there is a ball involved, I want to play it. Football, baseball, basketball, golf, tennis, even ping pong, I love it all. God has gifted me to be at least average in most sports. No, I will never be the best on the field or the court, but I can usually hold my own and not make a complete fool out of myself. Notice I said usually. However, that is not the case with all of the activities I have partaken in throughout my life.

I was in sixth grade, it was almost Thanksgiving, and our teacher had a fabulous idea: everyone in the class will make a turkey out of paper, and we will hang them on a bulletin board for all of the parents to see when they come visit the school for our fall festival. The idea was simple: place your hand on a piece of paper and cut around your hand to make a hand-turkey. After that, we were given some easy-to-use craft accessories to decorate said turkey. How hard could it be?

Well, apparently, I am not very gifted when it comes to arts and crafts. We started the project around 2:30 p.m. and school ended at 3:30 p.m. The project was supposed to take no more than 10 minutes, and then we would have 50 minutes to work on homework before heading home for the day. The majority of the class (and by majority, I mean everyone except for me) was finished by 2:45. Me? I still couldn't cut the thing. I tried four different times and each time I could not even cut a simple hand-turkey. The clock said 3:15 and at that point I was worried I might be spending the night in the classroom: every kid's worst nightmare. Noticing my pitiful struggle, my teacher walked over and decided maybe I needed some help. She then helped me cut the outline around my hand. Reminder, I was not six years old, I was in sixth grade. The hand-turkey was finally cut out, and all I had to do was decorate it. Well, that did not go too well either. The task was clearly impossible for me to complete, so I hung up my distinctly deformed "turkey" on the board and tried to hide it behind some of the other well-done turkeys. My parents, whom I love and have a fantastic relationship with, saw the turkeys and immediately picked out which one was mine. We had a good laugh that night. We still laugh about it to this day. God had obviously not gifted me in the area of art.

The reason I share this story is this: what if after that I said, "I want to be an artist." I could work ten times as hard as another kid who was gifted in arts and crafts and never be half as good! Also, I did not enjoy arts and crafts. To pursue art with my limited God-given potential in this area, and without any God-given passion in this area would have been nothing more than a waste of time. I could sit back and complain about the fact that my other acquaintances were gifted in art, or I could pursue the God-given gifts and passions that are evident.

This is something the world tends to do often. We compare ourselves to others who are simply more gifted than us in certain tasks and skills. Sometimes, we even compare ourselves to others who are gifted in areas where we are not gifted in the slightest. That would be like me comparing myself to Van Gogh. That would be foolish.

So maybe this side of comparison is easy for us to swallow. If we are bad at something, then why should we compare ourselves to someone who is good at that thing? Easy. However, the main form of comparison I see that tears humanity apart is the comparison of gifts and abilities with others gifted in the same areas as us. This is incredibly dangerous and not God honoring as it hinders us from excellence and keeps us from faithfully sharing our freedom in Christ with others.

By comparing ourselves to others, we are competing against creation. We are competing against something that is completely unique and unlike anyone or anything else. The Bible says in Psalm 139:14, "I praise you, for I am fearfully and wonderfully made. Wonderful are your works; my soul knows it very well." Again, in Romans 12:3-7 it says,

> For by the grace given to me I say to everyone among you not to think of himself more highly than he ought to think, but to think with sober judgement, each according to the measure of faith that God has assigned. For as in one body we have many members, and the members do not all have the same function, so we, though many, are one body in Christ, and individually members one of another. Having gifts that differ according to the grace given to us, let us use them: if prophecy, in proportion to our faith; if service, in our serving; the one who teaches, in his teaching; the one who exhorts, in his exhortation; the one who contributes, in generosity; the one who

leads, with zeal; the one who does acts of mercy, with cheerfulness.

Competing against creation is a slap in the face to the Creator because He made you with a specific, beautiful, and unique purpose and set of gifts. When we pin our gifts against another unique creation, we are comparing unequally functioning but equally beautiful gifts. We take away the beauty by focusing on the function which causes nothing but negative outcomes.

Instead of comparing ourselves to others and our organizations to other organizations, let's simply be excellent. If we do the absolute best with what God has given us, then we will be fulfilling our purpose, and most of all, bringing glory to our Creator. Set goals that push YOU to be YOUR best, not to beat your opposition. Instead of trying to produce more revenue and market share than your competition, simply be the best you can be and see how much profit and market share increases. Instead of worrying about how many calls the sales rep next to you is making, figure out how many you can possibly make in a day. Instead of wondering how much your friends are tithing, figure out how much time and money you can possibly give. It is a foolish task to compare sinners to sinners because we will always fall short even in "victory". It is much more fruitful for us to compare ourselves to the perfect standard outlined in Scripture, which allows us to always have something more to strive for and work for.

This might seem too simple and cliché, but I ask you to take a look around at your world today. Why do you drive the car that you drive? Is it because it is the vehicle you can afford, or is it to impress people on the open road that you have never met and will never meet? Why do you constantly open your phone to see how many likes your posts receive on social media? When you receive your sales reports for the month, are you comparing yourself against your previous best, or are you seeing what the other sales reps in the department are doing? Are you looking at how many new members the church on the other side of town has compared to yours? Do you slyly figure out how much money your friends and co-workers are making? If it was so "simple and cliché," then maybe we would stop playing the comparison game. However, since that is not the case, I think it is vital that we take it seriously.

As mentioned earlier, Theodore Roosevelt once said, "Comparison is the thief of joy." I would like to take that one step further and say comparison to the world is also the thief of excellence and achievement. If you lack joy, you will not be able to achieve your God-given potential. Like the late Steve Jobs once said, "Your work is going to fill a large part of your life, and the only way to be truly satisfied is to do what you believe is great work. And the only way to do great work is to love what you do."[3] The only thing we should be comparing ourselves to is what the Bible asks of us: our absolute best every single day.

The last misconception I want to tackle in this chapter is the idea that we can simply muster up the strength, courage, and determination to do this all on our own.

Acts 17:24-28 says,

The God who made the world and everything in it, being Lord of heaven and earth, does not live in temples made by man, nor is he served by human hands, as though he needed anything, since he himself gives to all mankind life and breath and everything. And he made from one man every nation of mankind to live on all the face of the earth, having determined allotted periods and the boundaries of their dwelling place, that they should seek God, and perhaps feel their way toward him and find him. Yet he is actually not far from each one of us, for in him we live and move and have our being.

God does not need us; We need Him. He will accomplish His eternal plan with or without us. However, He invites us to bear fruit and make His name known using the gifts He has given us.

John 15:4-5 says, "Abide in me, and I in you. As the branch cannot bear fruit by itself, unless it abides in the vine, neither can you, unless you abide in me. I am the vine; you are the branches. Whoever abides in me and I in him, he it is that bears much fruit, for apart from me you can do nothing." Apart from God, without His constant guidance, without His daily mercy, and without His renewing strength, we cannot accomplish what He has for us to do. No matter how much we life-hack, set goals, listen to podcasts, or make plans, without God, we will not have Biblical influence.

We are chosen by God and appointed to go and bear lasting fruit (John 15:16). We cannot bear this lasting fruit if we are not abiding consistently in our life-giving vine through God's Word, prayer, and Christian community. Only through daily surrender to God's Will, can we partner with Him to make a lasting, eternal impact. Only through partnering with God in His eternal plan, can we find meaning and purpose in our careers. Every other goal will leave us empty and wanting more. There is nothing more exciting and life-giving than being daily surrendered to God's plan and viewing your career, your office, and your team as your ministry through which you can make an eternal impact. In a world of quarterly goals, let's choose to live with an eternal mindset instead.

If we can all put aside these distractions and misconceptions that are so ingrained into society, then true, Biblical excellence can be pursued, and eventually achieved. Before moving on to the next chapter, I ask that you take some time in reflection to see what misconceptions you need to put aside before you begin your quest to achieve all that God has called you to.

Chapter Two

What Does the Bible Say About Excellence?

When we talk about excellence in business and in our careers, there are so many thoughts that come to mind. It seems to me that a large portion of our thoughts and opinions when talking about and thinking about excellence in the workplace and in life are the benefits of excellence, not necessarily the excellence itself. Later in this book I will discuss the benefits of becoming excellent and achieving success, but for now, let's look at the process of developing excellence from the ground up. To do this, we must start where all Truth begins: God's Word. 2 Timothy 3:16 says, "All

Scripture is breathed out by God and profitable for teaching, for reproof, for correction, and for training in righteousness."

In order for us to move forward, we must mutually agree that no matter what the world says, the Bible will be our foundation from which we begin our thought processes and make logical decisions. Yes, there are fantastic other sources out there besides the Bible that discuss hard work, successful work practices, and other topics like this. We will definitely use real business-world examples throughout this book, but those examples are only used to support what the Bible already says, not the other way around. It is always Bible first, culture second. We must keep that in mind moving forward, or we will be on two completely different wavelengths.

This may all seem basic, but it is vitally important. Sure, it is easy to say, "Yes I believe that the Bible is the Truth!" Then, a new article comes out that says something opposing the Word of God, and it sounds good. Maybe people we respect are backing the article, study, or sentiment. We may not look at that article and toss out all of the Biblical understanding that we have received, but we may start to do something even worse: add our opinions to God's Truth. This idea of adding to or taking away from the Word of God is not one I would suggest. The moment we start adding and/or taking away from the Truth outlined in the Bible to fit a popular narrative that sounds logical to our sinful, human minds, sin and failure are bound to follow. Proverbs 30:5-6 says, "Every word of God proves true; he is a shield to those who take refuge in him. Do not add to his words, lest he rebuke you and you be found a liar." For us to be successful and pursue Biblical excellence, we mustn't add our opinions to Biblical Truth. To be honest, why would we want to? It would be the same as a movie-goer watching the first five seconds of a movie and telling the director how they should have made their movie. It is illogical at best and utter blasphemy at worst.

As mentioned previously, before we talk about the results of excellence, we must look at and truly understand the process of what it takes to be excellent. Excellence cannot simply start one day out of nowhere. It is a process that takes time and starts deep within your mind, heart, and soul. At the beginning of human existence, in the Garden of Eden, when everything was perfect, there was work to be done. Work has existed since the dawn of creation. Therefore, work is not bad, but an absolutely good and holy activity when done the right way. However, because of sin entering the world, the mindset around work has been completely changed from a perfect idea to a fallen one. Where work used to be perfect, we will now experience "pain" and "toil" while working.

Genesis 3:17-19 reads,

> And to Adam he said, 'Because you have listened to the voice of your wife and have eaten of the tree of which I commanded you, 'You shall not eat of it,' cursed is the ground because of you; in pain you shall eat of it all the days of your life; thorns and thistles it shall bring forth for you; and you shall eat the plants of the field. By the sweat of your face you shall eat bread, till you return to the ground, for out of it you were taken; for you are dust, and to dust you shall return.

Where work used to be a gift from the Lord, we now view work as a curse. Maybe this is the reason, according to a Gallup poll, that 85% of people hate their jobs.[1] According to an article written by Karl Thompson in ReviseSociology, "35% of your total waking hours over a 50-year working-life period assuming 8 hours of sleep a night" will be spent working.[2] As Christians, how can we justify "hating" 35% of our time over a 50-year period? That is completely unbiblical and a tragedy to say the least. I would venture to say that it is because we are not pursuing excellence. We are dreaming of the clock striking five so we can get home to our family, go to church, spend time with friends, pursue hobbies, and "actually live out our purpose." Who are we to say what time of day our purpose begins and ends?

The scary thing to me is that we think our work does not serve a purpose. We think it is simply a way to collect a paycheck to fund what God actually wants to do through our lives. This is a lie. God does not tell us to go and make disciples 65% of the time, then use the other 35% of our lives to make money and work. We are called to make disciples 100% of the time, no matter where we are, no matter what we are doing. If you hate your job, I would ask that before you complain about your boss, your company, the economy, or your co-workers, that you take a deep, hard look at yourself and your own heart first. Have you been giving your best effort at work as unto the Lord? If you were, and you attached a Biblical purpose to your job, the anger and hatred you feel towards your alarm clock in the morning might diminish and your feet might hit the ground a little more quickly. Like Woodrow Wilson once said, "You are not here merely to make a living. You are here in order to enable the world to live more amply, with greater vision, with a finer spirit of hope and achievement. You are here to enrich the world, and you impoverish yourself if you forget the errand." Confining yourself to the mindset of simply making a living for 35% of your time on earth is selling others short, selling your life short, and even selling eternity short.

As God's children, there is no reason to hate what we do for work or give anything less than our best. We are on a mission! How can we possibly accomplish that mission if we are known around our offices as the negative, underachieving, gossiping employees? How much more influence could we have if we were known as the always positive, hardest working, top performing employee in our companies! This is what we should all strive for. If we are going to share the Gospel everywhere at all times like we are called to do, our behavior should back it up. We should look different from the world. Our bosses and coworkers should look at us and say, "How is she always getting so much done? How is he so positive? Why is she so nice? Why do his clients like him so much?" The answer to every single one of these questions is a massive door that is wide open just asking for you to share the Gospel. I don't know about you, but I would not want life advice from the coworker who is at the bottom of the sales board, complains about the boss, complains about their kids, speaks negatively about society constantly, and talks about how much they wish they worked somewhere else.

Imagine showing up for a serious surgery at the hospital. You are in dire need of this surgery to save your life. You arrive and are told the doctor is not in yet and is running late. The doctor walks in an hour late and immediately tells you how tired they are of being a doctor. They then start complaining about the nurses and other doctors. They then tell you that this is their least favorite kind of surgery and that they have the lowest success rate of any of the doctors in the entire nation. They then ask if you are ready to be put under anesthesia to begin the surgery. What would you say? Most likely you wouldn't say anything and would simply run out the front door and go to a different doctor. Going through that surgery with that doctor just doesn't make much sense and would most likely cause more harm than good.

We as Christians are just like this figurative surgeon all the time. We perform poorly at our jobs, complain about everyone besides ourselves, act lazily, and then wonder why people aren't interested in listening to what we have to say about eternity. When we behave like this, we look nothing like Jesus and deter others from wanting to know Jesus. When we work hard, point glory to God with a humble heart, possess an inexplainable amount of joy despite circumstances, speak highly of others, perform tasks that others would never want to do, offer to help our colleagues, and simply go out of our way to be of service, we look different in a way that draws in those who are searching. This is where the Gospel can be shared effectively.

Opportunity awaits those who are successful in the fields the Lord has placed them in. Wherever you are working right now, there are opportunities. Instead of thinking about your next job or when you can go home, make it your goal to earn influence through excellence with the heart of a servant. Be the person who does the extra task that no one wants to do. Be the team member who encourages the other employees. Be the boss who shows empathy for the team. Treat others like we would want to be treated. Treat others like Christ treats us.

God designed you and me to work from the beginning of time. For us not to do so is not only to dishonor God, but would also create a large hole in our very being that can only be filled through pursuing what we were created to do. I love the way Forbes contributor Marc Bodnick sums up this concept, "The secret sauce is in treating your job as if you love it, that is the surest way to lead you to a job that you actually love. Treat each day like drudgery, and you will toil forever."[3] This could not be more accurate. It reminds me of the famous C.S. Lewis quote that says, "Do not waste time bothering whether you 'love' your neighbor; act as if you did. As soon as we do this, we find one of the great secrets. When you are behaving as if you loved someone, you will presently come to love him."[4] Instead of moping around wishing you loved your job, act as if you did! Instead of wanting to love your co-workers more, act as if you did! Instead of wishing you did your work as unto the Lord, act as if you did! As simple as it sounds, a simple mindset shift can change everything and start you on the right track to achieving your God-given potential. The mind is an extremely powerful tool when used correctly and when used negatively. If we are not actively using it in a positive, God-honoring way and taking thoughts captive (2 Corinthians 10:5), it will automatically behave in a sinful, worldly way. To be sinful is to be normal, to be godly is to be intentional and focused.

Excellence begins with a shift in mindset, which then pours out of our minds through actions, which then creates excellence, which leads to success, which provides influence, which opens the door to pointing others to Jesus. Begin today with the interior workings of your heart and your habits of thought towards the concept of work. Decide that you will not become another cog in the corporate machine that hates Mondays and lives for the weekends. What a waste of time that would be. God has called you to play a specific part in His beautifully grand plan. Let's not waste another moment. What can you do today to take an intentional step forward towards Biblical excellence in your current circumstances?

Chapter Three
Examples of Excellence

In the previous chapters I explained what excellence truly looks like and what the Bible says about excellence. It is quite a difficult word to explain because it can take so many different forms. Excellence is something I see in my mind but cannot explain with my words without the use of simile and metaphor. To move forward in our understanding of excellence, let's look at four real-world examples of people who have lived out true, Biblical excellence in their field using their God-given abilities. The definitions of excellence listed previously apply directly to these individuals. I am not saying these individuals are perfect. They have made major mistakes, but so did David, a man after God's own heart, and so do you and I. Thankfully, even in our imperfection, God offers new mercies every day. Sometimes those who are the most excellent and have been given the most influence are those who have made the most mistakes and received the most grace. Let's look at a few examples of imperfect individuals who have been used by God to make a major impact and play roles in God's perfect plan.

The first individual I would like to examine is a man named Truett Cathy, the founder of Chick-fil-A. I was listening to a podcast recently interviewing David Salyers, the former Chief Marketing Officer of Chick-fil-A, who worked directly with Mr. Cathy throughout his entire career. He had started his career right after college working under Mr. Cathy, even though Chick-fil-A offered the smallest salary out of any of his job offers. He believed in the company, and in the founder. When asked what it was like to work under Truett Cathy, Salyers responded,

He was like a second father to me. I learned so much from Truett Cathy. Not only was he one of the best businessmen ever known, but certainly one of the finest men...What I thought a remarkable career looked like was to go out and make as much money as you could, as fast as you could, and retire early...Instead, by going to work for Truett, he introduced me to a concept I never would have imagined even existed. Instead of getting the job I could retire from at age 35, I got something far more remarkable. I found the job I wouldn't want to retire from. What Truett modeled every day was that work, when done right, is designed to be enjoyable, satisfying, rewarding, that great joy can come from work. Truett showed me if you love what you do, you'll never work another day in your life.[1]

Truett Cathy, when asked in his 80's why he still hadn't retired, responded, "Why would I stop doing something I love this much?" Cathy did not buy into the word "success" as described by the world. He did not simply put in his required hours with minimal effort to receive his paycheck and go home to start living his life. No. He saw work as a gift from the Lord, something that brought joy. Cathy used his God-given abilities to build a business that met worldly needs, while also providing for spiritual needs as well. This can be clearly seen in Chick-fil-A's philosophy which states, "Everyone's job at Chick-fil-A is to serve. No matter our title or job description, our reason for coming to work is to generously share our time and talents. Whether it's treating customers like friends, or serving our communities like neighbors, we believe kindness is a higher calling,"[2] or their corporate purpose which states, ""To glorify God by being a faithful steward of all that is entrusted to us and to have a positive influence on all who come into contact with Chick-fil-A."[3]

Through Cathy's hard work and consistent effort, Chick-fil-A has grown from a small fast-food company to a company that is known more for its service than its food. Since Cathy's death in 2014, the company has not slowed down a bit. It has won the award for Top Limited-Service Restaurant Chain in the country for four years in a row, generating more than

$10.4 Billion in 2018, all while being closed on Sundays.[4] The values of Cathy have truly been passed down through the business, affecting every single person who comes in contact with Chick-fil-A.

I am from Waco, Texas, so I would be remiss if I did not mention Chip and Joanna Gaines next. The Gaines duo is an incredible example of a couple who has used their God-given abilities to be excellent and creative in the marketplace while pointing all glory back to God.

The story of the Gaines family may seem like a classic "overnight success" story, but it is far from that. Growing up in Waco, I remember driving by the little Magnolia shop on Bosque Boulevard every week. It always had consistent customers, but was just another small business to the naked eye. Little did I know, that for years Chip and Joanna had put in excellent work on the homes that they renovated.

They never intended to be superstars. They simply wanted to be excellent in what they were doing, using the gifts God had given them. Then, one day a reality television producer happened to stumble upon a blog that featured one of Joanna's homes. The now world-famous show, Fixer Upper, was then started.

Because of Chip and Joanna's constant work, creativity, and pure excellence, they have grown their small shop on Bosque to one of the most recognizable brands nationwide. With the success of their television show Fixer Upper, they have been able to expand from their small shop on Bosque to a massive complex in downtown Waco. If you drive by Magnolia today, there is not only a steady stream of customers like in the past, but a booming economy full of visitors from around the world. I remember when the silos, the main focus point of the Magnolia complex, used to be an old, rusty building that was simply an afterthought. That is not the case anymore. In 2017 alone, the Magnolia Silos brought in over 1.6 million visitors.[5] Since Fixer Upper, Waco has been ranked as high as number two in the United States on TripAdvisor's list of "Travelers' Choice Destinations on the Rise."[6]

I promise this is not a "Come to Waco" advertisement. However, it is worth saying that the entire Waco economy has improved because of the excellence of Chip and Joanna Gaines. From small, local shop owners to nearly 18 million combined followers on Instagram and being thrust into celebrity status, it is safe to say life has changed for the Gaines family in the last decade.

We have seen time and time again many professing Christians become famous and then slowly fade away from faith in Jesus. This is simply not the case with the Gaines. They are open about why they do what they do. If you look at their social media profiles, their interviews, their books, and many other sources, they are always clear that Jesus is their Savior, He is the head of their household, and they will do whatever is necessary to stay close to Him. In 2018, Fixer Upper was bringing in over 75 million viewers as the number one rated unscripted series on cable television, yet they ended the show to focus on their family and pursue the Lord.[7]

Because of their excellence, they have been able to provide opportunities for others to know Jesus. One example of this is that the Magnolia Silo grounds now host "Church Under the Bridge," a body of Believers that used to meet every Sunday under a large bridge on Interstate 35, a massive road that passes through Waco. This church was founded with the purpose of bringing together people of all cultural, economic, and racial backgrounds under one roof to worship God the Father, Son, and Holy Spirit, even if that roof was a bridge. This church has changed the lives of countless individuals in the community, especially the lives of many in the homeless community. It is a beautiful picture of what heaven will be like.

Because of a large construction project, construction began on the bridges, and the church had no place to meet that could allow for such a large, outdoor gathering near downtown Waco every Sunday. The Gaines quickly jumped in and offered up their beautiful Magnolia complex to host the body of Believers. Now, if you drive by Magnolia on a Sunday morning, you will see a massive gathering of Believers from all different walks of life lifting up the name of Jesus.

In an interview with I Am Second, Joanna said, "I was made for a reason, and I need to let whatever God has created me for…be known. I don't need to stay hidden."[8] Matthew 5:14-16 says, "You are the light of the world. A town built on a hill cannot be hidden. Neither do people light a lamp and put it under a bowl. Instead, they put it on its stand, and it gives light to everyone in the house. In the same way, let your light shine before others, that they may see your good deeds and glorify your Father in heaven."

The goal is not to be famous; the goal is to be faithful. When we are faithful to do what God has called us to do and use the gifts He has given us, we will be given divine appointments to share the Gospel. When Chip and Joanna Gaines were faithful to make Jesus known and pursue excellence all those years I used to drive by their little shop, God was preparing a stage for them to proclaim the name of His Son to the entire world. Let's be faithful in the areas God has placed us right now. Let's allow our light to shine so that our workplaces, our communities, and the world may see our heavenly Father.

The next individual I would like to use as an example is a man named Paul J. Meyer. Meyer was born the son of an immigrant to a family with hardly any money to their name. They may not have had money, but they had integrity, work ethic, and faith. Throughout Meyer's young life, he was told over and over that he inherited a fortune, not a monetary fortune, but a fortune of knowledge and wisdom through the gifts God had given him. His mother instilled in him the belief that everything he ever needed to know was either in the Bible or in his brain. He took this to heart and began changing the world from a young age, never settling for mediocrity.

Paul J. Meyer worked many jobs throughout his adolescent years including picking prunes. He would be paid a certain commission per box of prunes that he picked. Realizing that he set his own salary at a young age, he began working sixteen-hour days, even setting the record for most boxes of prunes picked at this local establishment: 101 boxes![9] This work-ethic combined with his belief in his God-given potential allowed him to set records everywhere he went.

When he was in the military, he broke nearly every fitness record there was. While most soldiers were simply trying to make it through training, Meyer was attempting to break records. He did not want to be an average soldier. He wanted to be the best!

When he was an insurance salesman, he broke the record for most sales ever completed by a salesperson at his agency. He was also the youngest member ever of the Millionaire's Round Table. Meyer's work ethic, attitude, and integrity preceded him everywhere he went. Because of what he had done and how he had done it, no one questioned his values. After a while, he had developed such a reputation for success and integrity, that he founded his own company, Success Motivation Institute in 1960, and Leadership Management International in 1966.

He founded these two companies with the goal for Success Motivation Institute and Leadership Management International to, "Develop Leaders and Organizations to Their

Full Potential." One might say Meyer accomplished his goal and then some.

He began authoring and leading personal and corporate leadership and motivational programs, which are now translated in almost 30 languages and taught in over 80 countries worldwide![10] Each program is backed by the belief that every person has untapped God-given potential. These programs have been facilitated to millions all over the globe for over 60 years. Think of all the lives, families, companies, and societies that have been impacted because one man was faithful to use the gifts God had given him. He could have become another statistic, but instead, he broke the mold and changed the world, all while pointing everyone he came in contact with to Christ.

Meyer's outlook on life can quickly be summed up by his most famous quote, "Whatever you vividly imagine, ardently desire, sincerely believe, and enthusiastically act upon, must inevitably come to pass!" Habits of thought create attitudes, which create desires, which create actions, which create success, which create influence. It is all part of a process that Meyer lived throughout his entire life.

Sure, Meyer achieved financial success. However, one of his personal goals was to always give away more money than he thought would be a comfortable amount to give. I have personally heard hundreds of stories from pastors, missionaries, parents, and students who were struggling to survive, pay their bills, afford medical treatment, or were simply going through a rough patch. These stories always end the same way: Meyer sending needed funds through a letter in the mail, placing a letter on a doorstep with the necessary amount inside, or meeting with these individuals in person and handing them a blank check. Always accompanying the financial resources was the Gospel of Jesus and the value of eternal security by putting faith in Jesus. Meyer was able to give a total amount of more than $75 Million to dozens of organizations and thousands of individuals during his lifetime.[11]

Again, the goal of being excellent is not to earn money or fame. However, when we pursue excellence for the purpose of God-honoring influence, we will live with an open hand in regards to the resources God blesses us with. We are able to use those resources to point more people to the Gospel of Jesus, whatever those resources may be.

The last example of Biblical excellence I would like to look at in this chapter is a name you are most likely familiar with if you follow sports, Tim Tebow.

Tim Tebow grew up in a Christian home and had a great family that raised him well. Many can say the same thing, but not many have had the same result. What has set him apart?

In college at the University of Florida, Tebow was known for his work ethic. He set himself apart from others in the world of collegiate athletics through his play on the field, his workouts in the gym, and his passion for the Lord. It was noted during his time in college that trainers would have to limit Tebow on how much weight they would allow him to lift during workouts.[12] He would not be limited to the amount that a normal quarterback could lift and kept trying to push himself further to make himself better. He eventually was lifting so much weight, that the trainers were unsure of what would happen if he continued. This is the type of man Tebow is in every area of his life.

After a brutal loss in college, Tebow was quoted on live television as saying, "To the fans and everybody in Gator Nation, I'm sorry, extremely sorry. We were hoping for an undefeated season. That was my goal, something Florida's never done here. But I promise you one thing, a lot of good will come out of this. You will never see any player in the entire country play as hard as I will play the rest of the season, and you will never see someone push the rest of the team as hard as I will push everybody the rest of the season, and you will never see a team play harder than we will the rest of the season. God bless."[13]

After this quote, Tebow led the Gators to a 10-game winning streak, an SEC title game victory, and ultimately a national championship. He practiced what he preached, and the world took notice.

This carried over into his life after college athletics. Although he was never as successful in the pros as he was in college, he still put in more work than anyone else and had the right attitude. He was once chosen as the hardest working player in the NFL by Sports Illustrated in 2012.[14] This made Tebow arguably the most famous backup quarterback of all-time. He was not even playing in games, yet the media and the public were always looking for a quote from him.

Even after his dreams of playing professional football had started to fade, he was still quoted as saying, "Regardless of whatever I do, I know what my purpose is: to make a difference in people's lives."[15]

He has stayed true to those words. Tebow has now authored four best-selling books, one of which was named the 2017 Christian Book of the Year.[16] These books have helped countless people all over the world and allowed Tebow to open up a foundation called Night to Shine. This foundation throws proms all over the nation, and the world, for children and teenagers with special needs and allows them to have their own night to have fun, dance, and be surrounded by loved ones who simply wish to celebrate them. This ministry has impacted the lives of so many children with special needs, their families, and their loved ones. Although Tebow never won a Super Bowl or an NFL MVP, he has fulfilled his purpose of making a difference in people's lives.

On top of all of this, Tebow is now actively working with his wife, Demi-Leigh Tebow, to end sex trafficking around the world. Through the influence Tebow has because of excellence on the field, he is now able to shine a major light on the horrendous sex trafficking epidemic that is happening in every corner of the world today.

Tebow now also preaches at events like the Passion Conference that is led by Louie and Shelley Giglio in Atlanta, Georgia every year. Whether he is speaking to teammates in a locker room, to a child at Night to Shine, to an interviewer, or to a stadium full of people, Tebow faithfully, consistently, and excellently shares the Gospel.

These are just four examples of Christians who have used their God-given potential to impact the world on a global scale. Imagine if these people had not used their gifts. How many people would have not been reached? How many lives would have not been changed? How many lives are you currently not reaching because you are not using the gifts God has given you?

I want to now challenge you to take a step back and look at your own life. The mission of this book is to help you see what can happen if every Christian in every industry used their talents to their fullest potential to then gain influence to share the Gospel with more people. That is the goal. However, not every single person will be a CEO, a professional athlete, or a celebrity. The goal is not to become famous, but to use the influence that you are given to point back to Jesus. No matter the stage of our career, what our career choice is, or how much influence we have, we must continue to strictly boast in the saving death and resurrection of our Lord and Savior. Maybe more influence will come, maybe it won't. Either way, every person who knows you and is influenced by you should know that Jesus died for them and loves them.

In Matthew 5:9, Christians are called to be peacemakers. Notice we are not called to be peacekeepers, but peacemakers. In today's society where it is clearly seen that we are more divided than ever before not only as a nation, but as an entire world-wide society, peacemakers are needed. Now more than ever, it is absolutely vital that Christians are maximizing their influence to bring about peace through the only message that can truly bring lasting unity: The Gospel.

Remember the words of Luke 6:38, "Give, and it will be given to you. Good measure, pressed down, shaken together, running over, will be put into your lap. For with the measure you use, it will be measured back to you." This is not the prosperity Gospel. This is not "do more so you can earn more." This is a message telling you to do excellent work for the sake of Christ and others, not for yourself. Give with the gifts you have been given, maximize your God-given potential, and trust God to do the rest. The second most selfish thing you can do is keep your God-given gifts to yourself. The number one most selfish thing you can do is not share the Gospel with those over which you have influence once you have used your God-given abilities. It will be hard, and there will be much more suffering than if you played it safe for your whole life. However, it will all be worth it. This life is but a vapor (James 4:14), and the eternal impact of following God's plan will always outweigh short-term earthly struggles. Who is an example of Biblical excellence that you have witnessed in your life? What made them Biblically excellent?

Part Two: Why Should You Be Excellent?

Chapter Four

Modeled for You and Me

Throughout the book so far, we have covered the topic of what excellence looks like. In the words of Simon Sinek, "People don't buy what you do. People buy why you do it."[1] I believe this to be true in business and even more so in life. So, for us to move forward, we must tackle the question of why we should even desire excellence. I would like to do that now.

In the previous chapter, I went through a few different real-world examples of excellence. This type of excellence is rarely seen in today's modern society, but it was modeled for us in Scripture time and time again. The Bible is full of average people doing extraordinary things simply because they did what the Lord called them to do. They said yes to their calling, put in the hard work, and trusted God to provide the rest.

Think of King Solomon for a moment. He was, and still is, considered one of the wealthiest and wisest men to have ever lived. He did not achieve this status by simply sitting around and hoping for society's problems to go away. He worked to grow in wisdom and consistently asked for wisdom. 1 Kings 3:5-9 says,

> At Gibeon the Lord appeared to Solomon in a dream by night, and God said, 'Ask what I shall give you.' And Solomon said, 'You have shown great and steadfast love to your servant David my father, because he walked before you in faithfulness, in righteousness, and in uprightness of heart toward you. And you have kept for him this great and steadfast love and have given him a son to sit on his throne this day. And now, O Lord my God, you have

made your servant king in place of David my father, although I am but a little child. I do not know how to go out or come in. And your servant is in the midst of your people whom you have chosen, a great people, too many to be numbered or counted for multitude. Give your servant therefore an understanding mind to govern your people, that I may discern between good and evil, for who is able to govern this your great people?'

Solomon took an analysis of his situation and realized he was simply not prepared for the leadership position and influence he had been placed in at his age. Instead of becoming filled with pride and arrogance, backing away from the position, or buying into the idea of "fake it 'til you make it," Solomon humbled himself before the Lord and asked for wisdom. God was faithful to Solomon and granted him wisdom. When was the last time you simply asked God to give you wisdom in your profession or leadership role?

Another example is that of King David. David was not born with a silver spoon in his mouth. The "man after God's own heart" began as a shepherd who watched his flock of sheep continuously. In Scripture it is shared that David, while watching his flock, fought off bears and lions. That does not sound like someone sitting around gazing up at the sky to me. That sounds like someone who took his job seriously and completed his tasks faithfully. Because of this consistent work and integrity, when he was needed for much more, he was ready. Luke 16:10 says, "One who is faithful in a very little is also faithful in much, and one who is dishonest in a very little is also dishonest in much." If we are not pursuing excellence in our current job, our current financial situation, our current relationships, then why do we think God should bless us with more influence and more responsibilities?

A few verses later in Luke 16:13, Scripture says, "No servant can serve two masters, for either he will hate the one and love the other, or he will be devoted to the one and despise the other. You cannot serve God and money." It has been said that money magnifies the heart. One does not simply earn more money and become generous. One does not simply earn more money and become less angry. One does not simply serve the master of laziness, the master of money, the master of greed, etc., and receive more opportunity for influence for the Gospel. "Commit your work to the Lord, and your plans will be established," says Proverbs 16:3. Long hours of work come before reward. It seems that today, society has it the other way around. We expect a reward before we ever actually break a sweat and get to work. If we want more influence, we must be excellent and faithful in our current responsibilities. As we are faithful in the parts of God's plan that He has made known to us, He will begin to make the currently unknown parts of His plan known and understood. If we will not listen to, obey, and follow the known Will of God, why should God make known to us His unknown Will?

Another example we can draw from Scripture is that of Daniel. He grew up as a slave in Babylon after being captured by King Nebuchadnezzar. Most would simply ask, "Why me?" and be angry at God. Not Daniel. He accepted the situation he was given, disposed of any victim mentality he could have had, trusted God, and was eventually promoted to a position of authority under King Nebuchadnezzar. It was through the influence of Daniel that the kingdom ruled by Nebuchadnezzar was able to see some level of godliness in an otherwise godless culture.

Because Daniel was in a high position of authority, King Darius then befriended Daniel. However, there were many who became extremely jealous of Daniel's influence and position. Daniel 6:1-5 says,

> It pleased Darius to set over the kingdom 120 satraps, to be throughout the whole kingdom; and over them three high officials, of whom Daniel was one, to whom these satraps should give account, so that the king might suffer no loss. Then this Daniel became distinguished above all the other high officials and satraps, because an excellent spirit was in him. And the king planned to set him over the whole kingdom. Then the high officials and the satraps sought to find a ground for complaint against Daniel

with regard to the kingdom, but they could find no ground for complaint or any fault, because he was faithful, and no error or fault was found in him. Then these men said, 'We shall not find any ground for complaint against this Daniel unless we find it in connection with the law of his God.'

Daniel was so excellent and faithful in the position he had been placed, that not a single fault could be found, so they had to create a fault in conjunction with his love for the Lord. These individuals went on to set up laws that seemingly forced Daniel to pray to no one except Darius. However, because Daniel was faithful, he continued to pray as he always had to the Lord. Daniel was then arrested and thrown into a den of lions. I don't know about you, but it would be hard for me to stay faithful during a time of such persecution. However, Daniel accepted the punishment that was given to him without complaint yet again. While Daniel slept peacefully in the den of lions, knowing that God would protect and provide for him, as He had his entire life, those who had persecuted him were tossing and turning in their beds unable to sleep. The next morning, Daniel was released from the pit and the men who committed evil against Daniel were fed to the lions.

Solomon, David, and Daniel were faithful. They consistently worked hard, prayed hard, and trusted God in any circumstance or location that God had placed them. Because of this faithfulness, they eventually saw themselves in positions of influence. Although they all made mistakes along the way, they always repented and turned back to God, learned something from their mistakes, and moved forward. This is a beautiful picture of how we should act in our own work environments and with our own responsibilities.

If you read through Scripture, you can see one common trend among the individuals whom God showed favor: faithfulness. Those that God gave more influence to and used in His plan were those who stayed faithful to the God-given callings on each of their lives no matter what hardships or trials occurred. Faithfulness is not attractive, but it is the goal. There is a "hustle" culture out there today that idolizes getting no sleep, posting pictures on social media of your new car, flying on private jets, and going from meeting-to-meeting securing deals. This is not faithfulness, and this is not the Biblical hustle we are discussing. This is idolatry of self which is exactly what got Lucifer kicked out of heaven (Exekiel 28:11-19). When you are "hustling" to pursue self-sustained freedom and riches, you are actually getting closer to Satan, not God. When you are excellently faithful in every task and continuously asking God for help and wisdom, you are becoming more like Jesus.

The Gospels list story after story of Jesus performing miraculous miracles, speaking to large crowds, and pointing people to His heavenly Father. However, the majority of this was done in a three-year period. What about the other thirty years of Jesus' life on earth? What about all of the moments not listed during those three years of ministry with the disciples? Those years were most likely full of carpentry work, traveling by foot to new locations, one-on-one conversations, etc. Jesus was faithful when miraculous signs and wonders were occurring and when He was being beaten for sins He didn't commit, in the highs, the lows, and everywhere in between. If we are to be like Jesus, we need to be faithful during promotions and during firings, during long meetings and closed sales appointments, during the mundane and the awe-inspiring. It will make us more like Jesus and point more people to Him.

It is also important to remember that we will inevitably fail just like every example in this chapter besides Jesus. However, because of the faithfulness of Jesus to God's plan, we now have grace that covers us when we fail. No matter what you have done, what you are currently doing, or even what mistakes you may make in the future, you have the opportunity to choose Biblical excellence over worldly mediocrity from this day forward. Trust Him, be faithful, and take daily steps towards the callings God has placed on your life. Where your strength is too little, God will provide.

What ways can you embody the lives of Solomon, David, and Daniel in your current career today, this week, and this year?

Chapter Five
Wasting Time

According to a Pew analysis of Labor Department data, the average person worked over 1,800 hours last year.[1] 1,800 may sound like a small number to some of you. Keep in mind this is just the average taking into account all jobs and all professions. I am sure some of you are closer to 2,000 or even 3,000. However, for the sake of consistency, let's use the 1,800-hour figure found in the study.

If you analyze your last year of work, can you honestly say you used those 1,800 hours to use your God-given potential to do your work as unto the Lord? Were you the hardest worker in your department? In your company? If not, why? Did you have God-centered conversations or did you more frequently discuss the very sins that Christ died to eradicate? Were you known as an encourager to everyone you came in contact with?

What does it say about us as Christians if we are wasting 1,800 hours a year because we are leaving God at the door of our jobs? What does that directly say to those with whom we come in contact with at our jobs every single day?

Considering we spend so much of our time at work, our jobs should be a place where we spend a vast amount of our energy on sharing the Gospel in word and in deed. The sad reality among Christians is that if we truly sit back and think about how we spent our last year at work and in our professions, our actions and words probably don't line up with the Biblical example of excellence. If we lived and worked like we were supposed to, those 1,800 hours would be filled with the following:

- Working hard and diligently on every task
- Avoiding or even shutting down office gossip or relationship quarrels
- Listening well to those who open up about life outside of work
- Finishing projects enthusiastically and on time
- Speaking encouraging words to employees and co-workers
- Praying for others
- Admitting mistakes and asking for forgiveness
- Spending your time at work actually working and not on distractions
- Respecting others
- Treating every task as a way to glorify the Lord
- Asking to help others that cannot or will not help us in return
- Performing tasks outside of our job description solely to benefit others
- Capitalizing on opportunities to share your faith with others

Sadly, most people's 1,800 hours probably looked something like this:

- Gossiping about management or other employees
- Leaving as early as possible
- Complaining in person, over email, via text message, on Slack, etc. while at work
- Complaining at home about work
- Keeping your head down to avoid being asked to help with a task
- Doing the bare minimum and barely on time
- Constantly thinking you deserve better
- Scrolling on social media
- Avoiding co-workers who are difficult to have a conversation with
- Cutting corners on tasks
- Asking for a raise without doing exceptional work
- Not once speaking about anything other than surface level topics

- Not taking an interest in the lives of co-workers

Which list looks like a more accurate depiction of the last calendar year for you? Be honest with yourself. This is not a time to make ourselves feel good. This is a time to make a change so that we can have an impact on others. By knowing where we are, we can set a course to get us where we desire to go.

To be taken seriously in the world of business and in your career, you have to not only talk-the-talk, but also walk-the-walk. What good does it do for the worst worker and the lowest underperformer to tell someone about the one thing that changed their life? God can use anyone at any time, but if we are being honest with ourselves, most non-believers would probably think, "Why in the world would I want to be like you?" If we are miserable at work, always complaining and gossiping, and the lowest performer in our department, then what we have is far from desirable. We suddenly look like the rest of the world, not like someone who has been set free from all sin and unrighteousness or a city on a hill. Like Zig Ziglar once said, "The foundation stones for a balanced success are honesty, character, integrity, faith, love and loyalty."[2] If we truly want to make an impact and gain influence, we must put theory into practice through these characteristics and hard work.

A Christian in the workplace should lead by actions and attitudes, not simply words alone. Words are powerful, but I would argue actions are even more so. It says in Matthew 5:16, "In the same way, let your light shine before others, so that they may see your good works and give glory to your Father who is in heaven." Our actions point to He who is greater than us. If we are performing below-average, we are not honoring or glorifying our Father in heaven. Through excellent actions and intentional words, we can truly point people to Jesus through our careers.

It is widely accepted in the world of business to seek out those who are succeeding and find out what their "best practices" are. If you are producing high-quality results with a positive attitude, you will have best practices to share. When you share your best practices, they will be listened to and processed because they are coming from someone who has earned respect and influence, not a hypocritical jerk. There is not much worse than advice from a lazy underperformer.

Be someone who is sought after for wisdom and help. You can then coach and mentor others to reach their personal and business goals and help with life situations, all while sharing your faith during those opportunities. You are not going to have people asking for your help if you are the person consistently in need of assistance to perform your own required tasks. Go above and beyond and show others what working for a higher calling truly looks like. Crush the stereotypes that Christians are lazy know-it-alls through humble excellence and Christlike faithfulness.

One other aspect of excellence I want to touch on here is the importance of humility. If we are excellent and we are given influence to speak into the lives of others, we can quickly begin to think we are better than we actually are. Proverbs

16:18 says, "Pride goes before destruction, and a haughty spirit before a fall." When we apply pride to our excellence and in our influence, we will quickly come to a fall. There is no room for pride in the Body of Christ. Philippians 2:3 paints a clear picture of how we are to act with the influence that we are given: "Do nothing from selfish ambition or conceit, but in humility count others more significant than yourselves." We are to use our influence to serve others and point them to Jesus. 1 Corinthians 1:31 says that if we are to boast, let our boasting be only in Christ Jesus our Lord. When we gain influence through our excellence, we have the unbelievable opportunity to show the world what Christ-centered humility and service looks like. This is radically different than the world and provides divine opportunities to share the Gospel with those around us.

It is time for us as Believers to step up and decide to lead by example through words and actions. The world is looking for every possible excuse to denounce Christianity. I beg you: Do not give a reason to denounce Christ by acting like the complete opposite of how Christ lived. As Christians we are not only representing ourselves at our jobs, but the entire body of Christ. When you consistently act subpar to the calling of Christ and underperform in your job activities, you are not only hurting yourself, but also all of those who have gone before you and will come after you. Before walking in to work every day, take a step back and see the big picture. Paperwork is not your goal. Higher sales are not your goal. More profit at the end of the quarter is not your goal. Throughput is not your goal. Your goal is to use every single moment of your day for the glory of the Lord so that others may see His face through your life. It is hard to be negative with that thought pattern and constant prayer flowing through your mind and heart.

To a world that may not have read the Bible before, gone to church, put their faith in Jesus, or may have even been hurt by the church and Christians in the past, are you displaying the Good News through your actions and attitude every day in your profession?

Chapter Six

Whatever You Do

1 Corinthians 10:31 says, "So, whether you eat or drink, or whatever you do, do all to the glory of God."

In everything we say and do, we should be pointing others to Jesus. We do not receive a get out of jail free card while we are at work. Sure, your job may be stressful, you may work with people you do not necessarily enjoy, your boss may have unrealistic expectations, you may be objectified by unruly employees, and you may just wish you were at home (or anywhere else than work honestly), but God has a purpose for you right now where you are. Nothing happens by accident in the Kingdom of God. Every single moment is part of the grandest and most beautiful story ever told, and you and I have eternity's greatest opportunity, honor, and privilege to play a part in it.

On those days when you simply want to burst into tears at your desk, yell at a co-worker, quit and walk away, or just sit and be silent, remember your why. You were called to much more than a simple nine-to-five job. John C. Maxwell said it best in his book, "The Power of Significance: How Purpose Changes Your Life," when he said,

> If you want to make a difference and live a life of significance, you find your why. You need to tap into your purpose. I'm certain everybody has one. Your why is the life's blood of your ability to achieve significance. If you know your why and focus on going there with fierce determination, you can make sense of everything on your journey because you see it through the lens of why. Once you find your why, you

will be able to find your way. How do those things differ? Why is your purpose. Way is your path.[1]

When you are constantly aware of why you are where you are, you can find a way to be excellent and glorify the Lord. Although your job description may be simple, God's description of your role at that job is much different. Look for ways to go above and beyond in your work, in your conversations, and in your service to others. Lay off the horn in the parking lot, smile at the receptionist, ask how the janitor's day is going, bring coffee for the whole team simply because you care about them, open up your home to someone who is hurting, ask questions that dig deeper than simple semantics. These are cheap, simple tasks that the world simply does not do. Being like Jesus is not as hard as the devil makes it sound in our heads.

Speaking of why and way, I would be remiss if I did not mention the fact that we as Believers have been given a why and way by our Creator. Matthew 28:19-20 tells us our why when it says, "Go therefore and make disciples of all nations, baptizing them in the name of the Father and of the Son and of the Holy Spirit, teaching them to observe all that I have commanded you. And behold, I am with you always, to the end of the age." John 14:6 gives us our way when Jesus says, "I am the way, and the truth, and the life. No one comes to the Father except through me." We have been called to make disciples (our why) by pointing others to Jesus (the way), and we are not given a day off for that job. Remember, the average worker put in over 1,800 hours at work last year. In the previous chapter we were faced with the question of, "How did we spend those hours?" Again, be honest with yourself. Once you have done that, develop a plan of action to move yourself more towards the excellent influencer God has called you to be. Find a community of other Believers around you that can keep you accountable, constantly point you to Christ, be there to pick you up when you fall, and even to point out things in your life that don't currently look like Jesus. Share your plan of action on how you will spend your time at work glorifying the Lord with your community of Believers. Be honest and open. Make this a priority in your life.

I would challenge you not to read any further until you have done this honest assessment, developed a plan of action, and shared it with a group of Believers. It will change your life and way of thinking forever. If you do not know how to make a proper plan of action for this, then simply start here: Create a bullet point list with short phrases describing how you share the Gospel at work, how you show the Gospel at work, how your conversations point others to Jesus, how your work effort points others to Jesus, and how everything else you do in your career points people to Jesus. Then, make another bullet point list with "future description" phrases of how you want to act in the future.

Once you have done that, simply write small, daily steps down to get you from where you are to where you want to go. Make sure each step and goal align with Scripture. Take your list to the Lord in prayer. Share it with your community of Believers. Start doing it today.

If you take a hard, honest look at your current work situation, you will be able to find an unlimited amount of opportunities to be excellent. Start capitalizing on those today! There is no time to waste. Your job doesn't simply pay your salary, it is a calling of the highest importance to be the hands and feet of Jesus in your office to rescue lost souls from the grasps of hell. Most lost people will never set foot in a church building, but they are all around you in your office, in your classroom, in restaurants you eat at, at events, and in every other area of life you partake in. Thankfully the Church is not confined to a building on Sundays. Every moment of every day, including your 1,800 hours at work, you have the opportunity to be the Church to someone in everything you do.

This may seem like an overwhelming and impossible task. It is hard enough getting up for work in the morning, looking presentable, fulfilling basic job functions, conducting meetings, communicating effectively with your team, taking kids to practice, making dinner, cleaning the house, keeping the cars from breaking down, keeping up with the finances, and doing all of the other tasks in life. Adding this spiritual component to all of those tasks can seem like quite a weight on your shoulders. The good news is that you are correct. It is overwhelming and impossible for us to do on our own. However, we do not simply have to rely on our own strength and willpower to do what needs to be done and make a difference through excellence. We have a God that tells us "Do not be anxious about anything, but in everything by prayer and supplication with thanksgiving let your requests be made known to God" (Phillippians 4:6).

Make your request known to God that you need His power, peace, comfort, wisdom, and support to be excellent in your work and in everything you do. He will fill you up when you are empty and allow you to pour into others. You may feel alone at work, and prayer may seem like a far-off dream in your current work environment. Even if you are the only Christian in your company or department, you are not alone! The same power that performed miracles, healed the sick, and rose from the grave is there to give you a pick-me-up at the office to fulfill God's plan and will for your life and the lives of others. Lean into Him and use your God-given strength and your God-given potential to make a difference in your office and in all of those who are around you through your actions and attitude. Excellent actions and servant attitudes lead to influential opportunities.

I would also challenge you to change the way you think about what we have just discussed. You do not <u>have</u> to be excellent in everything you do to gain influence to point others to Jesus, you <u>get</u> to.

As flawed as we are, we have no business being involved in the perfect plan God has laid out for all of humanity. However, because He is full of grace and loves us, He allows us to play a part in His grand plan. This is an opportunity and a privilege of the Christian faith, not a weight on our shoulders. I would argue that doing what Christ has called us to do actually lifts weight off of our shoulders. Look at the Disciples. Even while being beaten, flogged, and sitting in prison, they were filled with joy and worshipful hearts because they were fulfilling the purpose God placed on their lives. The whips still hurt, the insults still left scars, and the jail cells were still cold, but the joy, peace, and worship were still real and overflowing. There is no task you could add or subtract from your schedule to make you less-busy enough to feel peace and joy. The only way to live a life of peace and joy that God desires for you is to surrender everything to Him and realize that you get to play a small part in His magnificent plan. When we view the places God has placed us as a mission field in which we <u>get</u> to do ministry, our outlook completely changes, no matter how difficult our circumstances may seem.

One thought that might be creeping into your mind right now is the fear of influence. For many of us, we may like the idea of flying under the radar at work. Being average at work allows us to keep to ourselves. I completely understand this feeling of fear and anxiety. It can feel crippling at times. However, I challenge you to remember the story of Moses. Moses could not understand why God would put him in a place of leadership, especially one that involved a large amount of public speaking to prominent figures in society. Moses had a speech impediment that crippled him with fear. God gave Moses the words to speak and the path to follow. All Moses had to do was have a willing heart to do what was necessary, go where God directed Him, and ask for help from God along the way. Do not worry about what you will say or do when influence comes, "for the Holy Spirit will teach you in that very hour what you ought to say," Luke 12:12.

So why should you be excellent? To bring glory to God in all you say, think, and do. By using our God-given gifts, we can point others to Him. You have been uniquely designed with a purpose and plan in mind. Inactivity is not what you were designed for. Through hard work, faithful effort, and prayerful surrender, the plan God has for your life will be put into motion. Do not fall into the trap of laziness and ineffectiveness. You have been created for much more than a life of mediocrity. Use this short time on earth to have a massive impact on eternity through your gifts and talents. You will be happy you did. Do not worry about the worldly implications of following God during your 100 or so years on earth. Focus on the heavenly, eternal ramifications of using your time on earth to follow God knowing that your first billion years in heaven will be glorious. What are gifts and talents that God has given you that you are currently not using to point others to Him?

Part Three: How Can You Be Excellent?

Chapter Seven

The Balance Between Excellence and Perfection

Winston Churchill once said, "Perfection is the enemy of progress," and I couldn't agree more with that statement. You have probably heard the term "Paralysis of Analysis" at some point in your life. At different points in our lives and careers we have all probably fallen victim to this type of perfectionism.

There is a massive distinction between doing your due diligence and perfection. Think about buying a car for a moment.

Let's say you were looking to buy a slightly used car that was reliable and would last a long time. You would go online, do some research, look up the top two or three vehicle models that fit what you are looking for. Then, you may decide you want a certain color, under a certain amount of mileage, under a certain price-point, etc. These are all very wise things to research before making a large purchase like a car. You then go to the dealership and tell the salesperson that you want a black car with low-mileage that is under a certain price point. The sales representative takes you to a few different models. You analyze the different features, make sure they work well, test drive them, maybe take them to a mechanic for a second opinion, and decide which one you want that is in your price range. You make the purchase, and drive off into the sunset happily ever after.

Now, I definitely skipped over some things in this scenario, but it is relatively similar to the way you and I will most likely buy a car. You do the research, ask some questions, test it out, make the purchase, and move forward. This is how we should be in our lives. We should analyze our decisions to make sure they are wise, ask necessary questions, test out our theories with Scripture, maybe even get second opinions from trusted advisors in our Christian community or small group, and then move forward. This would, mostly, lead to excellent decisions. This is excellent. Now, let's look at what perfectionism looks like when buying a vehicle.

You spend a couple months researching what make, model, and year you want your vehicle to be. You then go to the dealership when it is closed and walk around the lot to look in the windows of locked vehicles, not exactly sure what you are looking for. You do this a few times. Then, you come back during business hours and speak to a representative. You ask to test drive five different models. You test drive all five and go home to think on your decision. You then make a pros and cons list of each vehicle. You don't sleep because you are so stressed about your decision. You go back the next day and decide you want to test drive them all again. However, while sitting in the waiting room, you see an award on the wall that says another model just won an award for best-in-class safety. You then ask if you can test drive that car as well. You test drive all six, go home, and reevaluate your pros and cons list. Once again: no sleep, lots of stress and even more negative what-ifs bouncing around in your mind. You go back the next day and ask if you can see all of the same cars, but in white instead of black this time. You then ask if you can test drive all of those even though just the color was changed. You then ask if you can have a mechanic look at all of the black cars and all of the white cars. The mechanic charges by the hour so you spend a pretty penny on analyzing all of these vehicles. You finally narrow it down to two cars. You decide to take one more week to decide which car you would like. During that week you read every article you can find on each car. You go in to test drive the cars again. You then ask if you can sleep on it for just a few more days. You come back to buy the car you finally know you want, and it had just been purchased the day before.

Now, I hope you are a little bit frustrated reading that paragraph. I for one am frustrated just writing it! I know it is a little over the top, but isn't it exactly what we do every single day with different situations? God has called us to be excellent and go make disciples. However, when we are given the opportunity, we have to analyze every possible outcome that could potentially occur by simply using the gifts God has given us to do His will. We cover up our perfectionism with statements like, "I don't want to sound too pushy with my faith," "I don't want to sound too religious," "I deserve a break," "I'll never be as good as that person," "It's just not my calling," and many more! All the while, God is just asking us to trust him and go do something. 2 Thessalonians 3:10-12 says, "For even when we were with you, we would give you this command: If anyone is not willing to work, let him not eat. For we hear that some among you walk in idleness, not busy at work, but busybodies. Now such persons we command and encourage in the Lord Jesus Christ to do their work quietly and to earn their own living." We have clearly been called to work, and to do our work well. We are not called to over-analyze, but use the minds and gifts God has given us and with the help of the Holy Spirit to make wise decisions and take focused, intentional action.

In a Desiring God article written by Jon Bloom, he says:

> What we call perfectionism is not the same as the pursuit of excellence, though sometimes the lines can blur. When we pursue excellence, we're determined to do something as well as possible within a given set of talent, resource, and time limits. But perfectionism is a pride or fear-based compulsion that either fuels our obsessive fixation on doing something perfectly or paralyzes us from acting at all — both of which often result in the harmful neglect of other necessary or good things. What's behind our perfectionistic tendencies? We're complex beings, so it's rarely just one thing. In unusual cases, its primary cause is a clinical disorder or spiritual bondage. But as a rule, perfectionism nearly always has its roots in our desire for acceptance and fear of rejection. It can be the garden-variety, pride-fueled, general fear of what people will think of us, or it can be a crippling, conditioned fear of failing instilled into us by an abusive past or present authority figure. And if we're

honest, sometimes it's a convenient excuse not to do something hard. In other words, it's not really perfectionism, but indulgence wearing a disguise. Perfectionism is a common-to-man temptation we all face in our fight against sin. And the wonderful news is that God wants us to live in freedom from its tyrannical rule over us.[1]

Bloom goes on to discuss the often-misquoted verse in Matthew 5:48 which says, "You therefore must be perfect, as your heavenly Father is perfect." This verse can seem almost like a call to be a perfectionist. However, that is not the case at all. In Matthew 5:17, Jesus says, "Do not think that I have come to abolish the Law or the Prophets; I have not come to abolish them but to fulfill them." Bloom then says, "Jesus came to perfectly fulfill on our behalf God's demand on us for perfection." Yes, we are called to be perfect. However, because of Jesus' sacrifice for us on the cross, we are now conjoined to Him in all we say and do. We no longer have to be perfect, because Jesus was perfect and took on our sin and shame. Jesus has already purchased every ounce of our perfection. Therefore, all the pressure is off of us to impress others or live up to some unrealistic standard. We are now called to be excellent by understanding our sinful nature, leaning on Jesus, and using the gifts He has given us to their fullest potential. Where we fall short, He is there to help us up, and we will consistently fall short if we do not get started first.

This concept is perfectly displayed in Acts 18:24-28. It says,

> Now a Jew named Apollos, a native of Alexandria, came to Ephesus. He was an eloquent man, competent in the Scriptures. He had been instructed in the way of the Lord. And being fervent in spirit, he spoke and taught accurately the things concerning Jesus, though he knew only the baptism of John. He began to speak boldly in the synagogue, but when Priscilla and Aquila heard him, they took him aside and explained to him the way of God more accurately. And when he wished to cross to Achaia, the brothers encouraged him and wrote to the disciples to

welcome him. When he arrived, he greatly helped those who through grace had believed, for he powerfully refuted the Jews in public, showing by the Scriptures that the Christ was Jesus.

This passage of Scripture shows that we do not need to be perfect. Apollos was eloquent and competent in the Scriptures, but he was nowhere near perfect. He was excellent, not perfect. However, he boldly shared his faith with those around him. When he made mistakes, other experienced, more mature Believers named Priscilla and Aquila helped explain to him the Truth even more accurately. In the following verses, we see that even though not everything Apollos was saying was perfect, "he greatly helped those who through grace had believed." God doesn't ask for us to have the perfect script memorized when sharing the Gospel, or for us to have perfect outcomes when we do our work unto Him. He asks for us to do it boldly and excellently. When we take action in faith, God will help us understand the Truth more accurately. Even when we make mistakes, He will correct us through Scripture, through our community of

Believers around us, or through prayer. We are called to consistently be faithful and excellent in our actions, words, and in handling the Word of God.

During practice one day, a basketball coach had his team line up. He said, "We are going to practice the fundamentals today." They began practicing dribbling with their dominant hand, the most basic aspect of playing basketball. The team was made up of top collegiate basketball players, so some thought this practice was far beneath them and their skill levels.

The coach kept telling his players to pound the ball harder, keep your eyes up, dribble faster, etc. He kept pushing them until the simple drill of dribbling the basketball became difficult. The players began to lose their basketballs all over the court while trying to dribble as fast as they could.

When the team lost their dribble, the coach stopped the drill and said, "Very well done." The players asked, "Coach, we lost our dribbles. We failed. Why are you congratulating us?"

The coach responded, "That was the whole point of the drill. Sometimes we have done the fundamentals so much that we stop pushing ourselves to do them better. We simply do the minimum because we get bored with the basics. The basics are the deciding factor between being a good player and a great player. When you lost your dribble, you succeeded because you pushed yourself hard enough so that the basics were no longer easy to you. You got better, and that is the goal every day."

Are you faithfully working to do the basic functions of your job, the basic functions of loving others, the basic functions of following Christ better every single day? If they seem too easy and you have not failed in a while, is it simply because you have become stagnant and comfortable? To truly be excellent, you must push yourself out of your comfort zone and trust God to pick you up when you fall.

Another aspect of perfectionism goes back to the idea of fear. Since we belong to God and nothing can snatch us out of the palm of His hand (John 10:28), what is there to fear? Every ounce of fear you have stems from a lack of trust in God. Since Satan cannot snatch us out of God's hand, what's the next best thing he can do? Make us ineffective.

When I used to work in youth ministry, I remember many kids accepting Christ into their hearts at different points during my tenure. This was always a beautiful time of celebration and thankfulness for all that God had done. However, what usually followed was the new Christian being tempted like they had never been tempted before. Why is this? I venture to say it is because Satan had lost the war on that soul, so now he was going to distract them with little battles to keep them from focusing on the ultimate goal of making disciples and proclaiming that they were once blind but now see. When someone isn't saved, Satan has them right where he wants them. The moment your soul belongs to God, the evil one has lost. The only chance he has is making you ineffective in your day-to-day life. Do not fall into that trap! Know it is coming. The moment you start taking steps of faith towards Biblical excellence, something will happen that negatively impacts you. It happens almost every time. Be prepared for it in prayer, in community, and in Scripture to push through those times of terror. You may have to walk through some dark valleys, but the oasis on the other side is beautiful and worth it. Keep moving forward clinging to the ever-guiding embrace of our Father.

The last aspect of perfectionism I would like to discuss is what happens when we do move forward. Once you have finally gotten over your fear of failure, you will most likely fail! This is not too uplifting, but it is just the honest truth. Failure is part of growth. Henry Ford once said, "Failure is simply the opportunity to begin again, this time more intelligently." "Mistakes are merely steps up the ladder," as Paul J. Meyer put it. Like the story stated before about the basketball team, if you are not failing, you are simply not trying hard enough.

The best part about failure? As Christians, there is grace to cover our failures. Lamentations 3:22-23 says, "The steadfast love of the Lord never ceases; his mercies never come to an end; they are new every morning; great is your faithfulness." When we are attempting to use our God-given gifts, remember where they came from and the characteristics of the One who gave you the gifts. There is no need to fear.

Think about some of the greatest companies on the face of the earth for a moment. One example is Apple. We now know Apple as the company that created the likes of iTunes, the iPhone which most of the world has in their pocket right now, the Mac, iCloud, and many other technological advances that most mere mortals could never have even dreamed of creating. However, they were not an overnight success. Most businesses never are.

Steve Jobs and Steve Wozniak created the Apple II and released it in April of 1977. This is the computer that is said to have revolutionized the entire personal computing industry.[2] It was the first personal computer to have color graphics, gaming capabilities, extra slots for additions, and much more. People loved the Apple II and bought over 300,000 units.

Apple then released the Apple III which was nothing short of a disaster.[3] It was said to have been released too early, and sold only a mere 65,000 units. Apple was on the brink of an entire company breakdown. However, Jobs and Wozniak did not stop there. From this failure, the true masterpiece was born: the Mac. This is the computer that changed everything. Through one of the best commercial masterpieces ever seen during the Super Bowl of 1984, Jobs and Apple announced the Mac to critical acclaim.[4] This computer came with a monitor, a keyboard, and a mouse which was the first to truly use the now standard point-and-click system of computing. The Macintosh sold over 70,000 units in just 50 days! However, failure was still to follow.

Steve Jobs was fired from Apple on September 16, 1985. This decision proved to be a poor one for the company. This set back Apple, and it set back Jobs. Their relationship had been severely hurt, and both parties suffered. Instead of calling it quits, Jobs came back to Apple on September 16, 1997. Since 1997, think of the products the late Steve Jobs and Apple have released to the world. All of the world-changing products listed at the beginning of this section were released after the failures listed previously. Imagine if Jobs and Apple had called it quits after the failure of the Apple III, or after the downfall following the firing of Steve Jobs. We would have never had the products that have revolutionized all of civilization. Failure is nothing to be afraid of. It happens to everyone. It is what we do with failure that matters.

As Believers, failure is something we need not be afraid of even in the slightest. Romans 8:31 says, "What then shall we say to these things? If God is for us, who can be against us?" Do we truly believe that? If we did, we would not be afraid to take calculated risks in our businesses and in our lives. Some of the things we fear in life (loss of money, loss of fame, the future, death, etc.) are all mentioned later on in Romans 8:35, "Who shall separate us from the love of Christ? Shall tribulation, or distress, or persecution, or famine, or nakedness, or danger or sword?" It then goes on to say in verse 37, "No, in all these things we are more than conquerors through Him who loved us. For I am sure that neither death nor life, nor angels nor rulers, nor things present nor things to come, nor powers, nor height nor depth, nor anything else in all creation, will be able to separate us from the love of God in Christ Jesus our Lord."

If we can honestly say the love of God is our most valuable possession, then these verses put to death any thought that we should be afraid of failure in our jobs. We have absolutely nothing to fear. The weight has been lifted, and the price has been paid. We simply get to live in the freedom and grace of Christ's sacrifice for us.

This can clearly be seen in the life of Job. At the very beginning of the book of Job (1:21), he writes, "And he said, 'Naked I came from my mother's womb, and naked shall I return. The Lord gave, and the Lord has taken away; blessed be the name of the Lord.'" Job was a man who, according to the Bible, was "blameless and upright, one who feared God and turned away from evil. There were born to him seven sons and three daughters. He possessed 7,000 sheep, 3,000 camels, 500 yoke of oxen, and 500 female donkeys, and very many servants, so that this man was the greatest of all the people of the east." I am not sure what the value of his livestock was, but he was clearly a very wealthy and honorable man. It is safe to say that Job was on top of the world, and gave all of the credit to God. This is what Biblical excellence can look like. However, we must also remember what happened to Job even though he was an upright, excellent man.

Job lost his livestock, his wealth, his houses, and his own children. Take a minute to imagine this. Most likely, no one reading this will ever come close to the wealth of Job. However, imagine all of your current wealth, health, and possessions being taken away. Then, all of your family was killed. This would be incredibly painful and you might be angry with God. Then, multiply all of your possessions by about 100 and that is probably what Job went through. It is impossible to imagine, but easy to see how someone could be angry, confused, and depressed through this situation.

However, even through all of this pain and suffering, Job never cursed God or turned his back on Him. He always put His trust and faith in the Lord, knowing that He would provide. Sure, he was angry, in pain, and experienced many other negative emotions, but he never ran from God. Job knew that every single one of his possessions and good fortune came from God. If God chose to take that away from him, then he could not complain, because it was not his to begin with.

This is the type of attitude we should have while facing our jobs and lives. No matter what may come our way, what failures may occur, or what hardships may seem to defeat us, we must trust that God has His eternal plan for His Kingdom and our best interest at heart and will provide for us. Our job is to keep pushing forward and to continue using the gifts God has given us instead of focusing on the gifts that have been taken away. They are all God's possessions. We must be thankful for what He chooses to allow us to steward.

Living life this way allows a huge burden to be released from our shoulders. We no longer have to fear about the future. We no longer have to fear about what our boss thinks of us. We no longer have to fear about cutbacks or downsizing. We no longer have to fear about impressing our coworkers. All we are called to do is to do the best we can and be good stewards of the gifts given to us. The rest is up to God.

You are free to set lofty goals that push you to be your best, and not settle for comfort. If you fall short of your goals, you have a loving Father who is there to pick you up and keep you moving forward, no matter what the world says. When you feel like you cannot possibly keep pressing on, you have access to the greatest source of strength. When you are faced with tough decisions, you can flee fear and use your access to the Creator of wisdom and all things that are good to make your decision. You are free from the jail cell that is the sinful human mind!

I hope you can feel the weight being lifted off of your shoulders even as you read this. Live out this concept in faith at work and in your day-to-day life. Your stress levels will go down, and your results will go up. You can throw society's and your own unrealistic expectations in the trash and never look back. You are free from those weighty chains. What are some unrealistic expectations you have placed on your life that you would like to throw away? How can you live out excellence without being stuck in the fear of failure and perfectionism?

Chapter Eight

Faith Over Fear

Once we have made the decision not to be afraid because God is on our side, another thought begins to creep in. "Is this what I am actually supposed to do? Am I actually good at this? Is this actually my calling?" These thoughts can stop us in our tracks and cause us to be ineffective and go back to living in fear. We start to believe that we don't have what it takes to be excellent. We don't have faith that God will provide for us when we take a step in the direction that He is leading us.

In a book written by Norris Blount titled "Game Changer: A Playbook for Winning at Life," he says, "Ask yourself, 'Do I have what it takes?' The answer is, yes. You have exactly what it takes because you were made to do what God has planned. If every one of us knew today how many days we had left, how many hours and minutes, what would we do?"[1]

This is an extremely sobering and humbling thought process to have. If we take a step back and remember that our time on earth is the same as a vapor in the wind, our mindset begins to shift. We realize that we simply don't have the time to fear! We have a mission that must be accomplished and every second we are not living on mission and using our gifts to be excellent is another wasted second in our brief time here on earth. Those that have been the most successful throughout history are those that simply used the most of their time here on earth to be excellent and use their gifts consistently.

I challenge you to right now think back to the last time you overcame fear and put yourself in a position to make a difference with your gifts. Picture it vividly in your mind. When you got to the point of finally using your gift, what did you do? Were you crippled yet again by fear or did you push through the final wall of fear to excellence?

I remember reading about the singer Phil Collins' battles with stage fright throughout his career. He would be completely paralyzed by fear any time he was about to take the stage, no matter how many people there were in the crowd. His bandmates and manager would have to encourage him to get out there, and eventually he would.

Collins had seven number one Billboard hits throughout his career. Imagine if he had never gone out on stage because of fear. Imagine if he had never overcome his fear and taken the step out onto the stage in front of thousands of screaming fans. We would have probably never heard of him, and the music world would have never been blessed with some of the top songs in the history of music, specifically that incredible drum beat from "In the Air Tonight."

The reason I use Phil Collins as an example is because of three reasons:

1. What is your stage? What stage are you afraid to step into?
2. Whom do you have around you that will push you out on stage if you are crippled with fear?
3. What would the world look like if you took faithful step out on to the stage presented before you?

Let's look at the first question. Your "stage" could look like meeting in a boardroom, eating and having conversations at the dinner table with your family, giving a news interview, writing a book, preparing and speaking a sermon, teaching a class, volunteering at a non-profit, spending time with your children, mentoring someone younger than you, leading a small group or Bible study, and countless other things. I don't know what your stage is, but you do. I encourage you to take that faithful step out on to your life's stage. The "performance" may not be pretty at first, but once you do it a few times, it will continuously get better. Keep working at it and trust God to guide you when you need help. Trust Him and take the first step.

The second question is one that is incredibly important. If we take a look back at the story of Job, we can see that he did not have the best circle of influence around him during his struggles. His wife told him to "curse God and die," and his friends pestered him with questions regarding what sins he had committed to bring forth such terrible atrocities to his family and himself. If your group of "encouragers" looks like Job's, it may be time to find new friends. As Believers, we need to seek out those around us that are there to live out Romans 12:15 with us. The verse says, "Rejoice with those who rejoice, weep with those who weep." Does your inner circle look like this? If not, I encourage you to find a group of people that can rally around you and support you through the peaks and valleys of life. Find a local church to do the same. This is absolutely vital to being Biblically excellent.

The last question I asked previously is the one I want to focus on most. We will do so at the end of the book. For now, I want you simply to picture what your micro world would look like if you took a step in faith towards following God's plan for your life and using the gifts He has given you. Don't spend any time thinking about the potential problems that could occur. Simply visualize the lives that God could impact through you and your gifts. This is the thought process needed to move forward in this book and in our lives.

One of my favorite quotes is from Lao Tsu and says, "To know and not to act is to not yet know." That is the cold hard truth. We know we should take action. We know God has gifted us in different areas. The fact is, we are simply not doing anything about it! James Clear once said, "You don't need much motivation once you've started a behavior. Nearly all of the friction in a task is at the beginning. Motivation often comes after starting. Find a way to start small. Objects in motion tend to stay in motion."[2] You simply must get started in faith and trust that God will guide you as you continue moving forward.

Results may not come immediately, but they will come with time as you continue using and fine-tuning your gifts consistently. John Wooden once said, "When you improve a little each day, eventually big things occur. Not tomorrow, not the next day, but eventually a big gain is made. Seek the small improvement one day at a time. That's the only way it happens – and when it happens, it lasts." Phil Collins simply had to get out on stage. That was his first step. Once he was out there, he gave the crowd an incredible show. He did not have to think about each lyric to each song or each movement he would make to be excellent. All he had to do was take the first step of getting in front of the crowd. The rest handled itself.

This is the same as the story of the talents found in Scripture. This parable is found in Matthew 25:14-30 and says:

> For it will be like a man going on a journey, who called his servants and entrusted to them his property. To one he gave five talents, to another two, to another one, to each according to his ability. Then he went

away. He who had received the five talents went at once and traded with them, and he made five talents more. So also he who had the two talents made two talents more. But he who had received the one talent went and dug in the ground and hid his master's money. Now after a long time the master of those servants came and settled accounts with them. And he who had received the five talents came forward, bringing five talents more, saying, "Master, you delivered to me five talents; here, I have made five talents more." His master said to him, "Well done, good and faithful servant. You have been faithful over a little; I will set you over much. Enter into the joy of your master." And he also who had the two talents came forward, saying, "Master, you delivered to me two talents; here, I have made two talents more." His master said to him, "Well done, good and faithful servant. You have been faithful over a little; I will set you over much. Enter into the joy of your master." He also who had received the one talent came forward, saying, "Master, I knew you to be a hard man, reaping where you did not sow, and gathering where you scattered no seed, so I was afraid, and I went and hid your talent in the ground. Here, you have what is yours." But his master answered him, "You wicked and slothful servant! You knew that I reap where I have not sown and gather where I scattered no seed? Then you ought to have invested my money with the bankers, and at my coming I should have received what was my own with interest. So take the talent from him and give it to him who has the ten talents. For to everyone who has will more be given, and he will have an abundance. But from the one who has not, even what he has will be taken away. And cast the worthless servant into the outer darkness. In that place there will be weeping and gnashing of teeth."

At the beginning of this passage, we see that three different servants have been given a certain set of talents according to their ability. This is a direct correlation to what God has entrusted to us. God has given us many giftings and talents to use for His glory. Some people have an unimaginable number of gifts, some are highly skilled at a few things, and some are specifically skilled at one certain thing. No matter the number of skills and gifts, God has given all of us something that we have been entrusted with to use for His glory and His plan.

The next part of the parable is where we tend to fall short in our own lives. Have we used the talents we've been given or simply hidden them? Are we using our giftings to go forth and make disciples in the arenas of life that we are in because of our talents, or are we content with keeping our giftings to ourselves for our own selfish gain? This is an extremely difficult objective. As humans, we desire comfort and security. It is our natural tendency. However, to do what Christ has called us to do, we must develop our talents and multiply them so that we can influence as many people as possible for the cause of Christ.

At the end of the parable, we see how seriously God takes what we do with what He has entrusted to us. The two servants who present their extra talents to their master are called "good and faithful." Not only are they congratulated by their master, they are then entrusted to steward much more. However, when the other servant, who was given little to begin with, presents simply what had first been entrusted to him, he is called slothful, wicked, worthless, and is cast into the darkness.

When we are faithful to use what God gives us to its fullest potential, God gives us more to use to make an even bigger impact. We are given more responsibility when we are responsible with what we have first been given. Instead of judging the amount we have been initially given, we must be faithful stewards of what we have been blessed with. Why should God trust us with more responsibility when we readily complain and are lazy with what He has already called us to steward? We feel as though we are entitled to as much as the next person, but that is simply not the case.

Imagine going into work and walking into your boss' office. You are supposed to be turning in a report on what you have accomplished over the last quarter. Instead, you tell your boss that you did not prepare your report because you were not happy with the work your boss had given you to do that quarter. Not only do you complain about this, you also bring up the department's top performer and complain about the fact that they are asked to do more than you. You demand that your boss give you just as much responsibility as your co-worker. You also ask for a raise.

What do you think your boss will do in that situation? Will they give you the raise and entrust you with more, or do you think they will kick you out of their office and fire you? I would venture to say we can all agree that you would be packing your things and loading them into your car before the day is over. What would your boss do with what you were initially entrusted with? They would give your work (and probably your salary) to the top performing co-worker you just complained about. Is this entire interaction your fault or your boss'?

Why is it so easy to identify the fact that this ridiculous scenario is our fault, but we do this every single day with God and continue to play the victim?

Does any of this sound familiar?

- "Why do they get to make so much money?"
- "How come they get to go on vacation?"
- "Why do they get to lead a small group at church?"
- "Why did they get the promotion?"
- "Why didn't I get to marry someone like that?"
- "Why don't my kids behave like theirs'?"
- "How come I didn't get selected for that project?"
- "Why are they married and I'm not?"
- "Why are they so talented at that and I'm not?"

I could go on and on, but I think you get the picture. People everywhere spend more time complaining verbally or in their own heads about others than they do being thankful for what God has already blessed them with. No matter what we are given, we want more. Once we are given more, we want what the next person has. The cycle never ends.

What is the root of this issue?

The root of all comparison and thanklessness comes down to a lack of faith and being controlled by fear. We don't actually believe that God has our best at heart. We believe we know more than God does about our lives. We think that if God would just let us be in charge of certain aspects of our lives, then everything would run smoothly. This lack of faith is seen throughout Scripture in almost every sinful act.

Since the beginning of time in Genesis, Satan's oldest trick has been to get us to think about what we don't have rather than what we do have. When we do that, we become paralyzed and fail to act on the giftings entrusted to us by God. We fail to be excellent, thus stripping us of all potential for influence. We are made ineffective, which is the best the enemy can do against those who have professed their faith in Jesus.

We are also controlled by fear when we have a lack of faith. We are scared of what the world will think, what the world will do, what those at the office will say, how our paychecks may be affected, that we will be called hypocritical since our own lives are anything but perfect, the fear of failure, and the list goes on. What fear is crippling you from pursuing excellence in the areas God has gifted you?

Chapter Nine

Who Could Be Against Us?

"What then shall we say to these things? If God is for us, who can be against us?" - Romans 8:31

In the workplace, fear is a very real aspect in our day-to-day existence. Work is stressful enough, but then you add imperfect people into the equation, and it becomes even more messy and stressful. There are a multitude of things we can worry about in regards to work, money, business, etc. Some of them could be downsizing, deadlines, a recession, technology, our position security, office politics, quarterly earnings, acceptance, career growth, the next raise, and much more. I'll stop before the list stresses you out too much. The fact is, imperfect businesses in imperfect offices being run by imperfect people will always have the potential to fail. If we let this fear overtake us and control our lives, we will become completely immobilized, thus disconnecting us from our journey of the pursuit of Biblical excellence for Gospel-centered influence.

This reminds me of college. The worst two words in the English language for a college student are "Final Exam." There were not many things more difficult than locking yourself away from all of the outside distractions to practically memorize a semester's worth of ideas and concepts. Now, if you prepared well, there was nothing to worry about. However, there were also those who prepared better than most but performed worse than most. Many of these people suffered from test anxiety. Test anxiety is the feeling of being overwhelmed when you sit down to take an exam. I'm sure we all knew someone like this in college. Most of the time, these people were incredibly smart, hard workers, and knew the information covered in class. When it came time for the exam, though, all of the knowledge would be completely washed out by fear and anxiety. This would cause their minds to freeze during the exam, not allowing them to perform well, utterly forcing them to fail the test.

This is what happens in our everyday lives as well. Many times, we become so crippled by fear, that all of the Truth of the Word that we know, all of the encouraging words we have heard, and all of our Christ-centered confidence are completely washed away in a sea of fear and doubt. We can't explain it, but we are helpless. We feel empty and we cannot do what we are supposed to do.

Now let's compare this idea to what life and work are like without fear. Without the fear of failure, of doubt, and of insignificance, we are free to work our hardest, try new things, and push ourselves to new highs even though we may fail. Failure simply becomes a step on the ladder to success, not a stumbling block. Imagine if the Wright Brothers, Nikolai Tesla, Thomas Edison, or Benjamin Franklin had quit after their failures. Think of all of the tools and ideas we use every day that have been developed by someone who failed time and time again. Some of the greatest thinkers and achievers of our generation had something to say about fear:

"You'll always miss 100% of the shots you don't take." - Wayne Gretzky

"What would life be if we had no courage to attempt anything?" - Vincent van Gogh

"Inaction breeds doubt and fear. Action breeds confidence and courage. If you want to conquer fear, do not sit at home and think about it. Go out and get busy." - Dale Carnegie

"Success is not final, failure is not fatal: it is the courage to continue that counts." - Winston Churchill

"Do not fear mistakes. You will know failure. Continue to reach out." - Benjamin Franklin

Those who have achieved the most with their God-given abilities have most often failed the most in pursuit of excellence. Knowing that God is on our side defending us, providing for us, protecting us, and calling us to live according to His purpose, there is no room for fear. To truly become excellent, we must come to terms with the idea that failure is not final.

Once we have overcome our fear of failure and have embraced our identity in Christ and the abilities with which He has blessed us, we can truly begin the process of taking action towards success. We should be completely filled with humble confidence as we make our daily commutes to and from work, to and from meetings, to and from networking events, and in any other aspect of life. Knowing who you are in Christ and trusting that He has a perfect plan for your life in accordance with His will and your gifts allows you to live with a newfound confidence that is impossible to experience otherwise. However, as we humans tend to do, we can still find a way to turn this Christ-centered confidence into something sinful. If we are not careful, we will begin to slowly forget that our gifts, abilities, and opportunities come from the Lord and equate our successes to our own doing. Soon enough, we will put our faith in our worldly abilities, and not in our Father in heaven, who gave us the abilities in the first place. If you have been around the church long enough, I am sure you can think of someone who started off giving all praise to God, but then slowly began fading away as they achieved more success.

What is God's outlook on pride versus confidence? In 1 Peter 5:5-6, it says, "Likewise, you who are younger, be subject to the elders. Clothe yourselves, all of you, with humility toward one another, for 'God opposes the proud but gives grace to the humble.' Humble yourselves, therefore, under the mighty hand of God so that at the proper time he may exalt you." In this passage, we see two things. One, God is strongly against those who are prideful. Two, for us to actually succeed and be exalted, we must humble ourselves first. This applies directly to our careers.

When we are at the office, if we walk around with a chip on our shoulder thinking we are better than the next employee and deserve more, God will oppose that. However, if we are the first to serve a colleague or a client, the first to lend a listening ear to someone who is hurting at the cost of answering a few emails, or the first to put an end to office gossip, God will exalt us to make His name known. This reminds me of the old saying, "Blowing out someone else's candle doesn't make yours shine any brighter."

The moment we begin to think about ourselves before God or others, we are treading into dangerous territory. 1 Corinthians 1:31 says, "So that, as it is written, 'Let the one who boasts, boast in the Lord.'" Every sale, every promotion, every account, every idea, every interaction, etc., are all a gift from the Lord. It would make no sense to brag about something that you did not do. It would be foolish for me to brag about Tiger Woods winning the Masters or Steve Jobs inventing the iPhone. The same applies when we use the gifts God has given us to complete works He has prepared in advance for us to do (Ephesians 2:10) and then attempt to take all of the credit. However, we can boast in the fact that God is good and everything He does is perfect. We can also be full of gratitude and thankfulness that He chose us to take part in His grand and eternal plan.

This is the key difference between pride and confidence. A confident Christian knows who they are in Christ, trusts that God has a plan for their life, believes that God has equipped them to impact people and live on mission in their specific community, and does not need to fear failure. Living with this mindset makes you stand out among the rest of the world. We can be confident in these things, thus allowing us to work harder and pursue excellence in our work and all areas of life.

When it comes to confidence versus pride, the bottom line is this: If we must think about ourselves, we should be thinking about how we can do the best job we possibly can to live out the mission God has called us to. If we are thinking or speaking about others, we should strictly be looking at ways to serve them. This is what Biblical excellence looks like. When our focus is on service, doing our jobs to the best of our abilities, and looking for opportunities to go above and beyond in every aspect of our lives and careers, eventually, influence will come with that. The sad reality is the world does not define excellence this way. Worldly excellence screams, "me first," when Biblical excellence asks, "how can I put you first?" Be confident that you are able to accomplish what God has called you specifically to do, but not prideful that you are better than someone else.

Think about salespeople for a moment. We have all dealt with the two kinds of salespeople: the commission-seekers and the servant-hearted individuals. When we have been forced to construct a deal with a pushy, money-minded, and selfish individual, we usually end up spending less, not spending anything, or at least leaving the deal vowing to never do business with that person again.

Now, think about the salesperson who went out of their way to serve you. They did not push the most expensive product or service on you. They refused to put pressure on you to act now or lose out on a once-in-a-lifetime offer. They asked personal questions to find out how they could specifically bring you the most value. When working with a salesperson like this, we usually end up finalizing a purchase with them and going the extra mile to refer a friend to them too. Applying the basic Biblical principle of putting others first translates into obvious career success. Sometimes even when we do the right things and treat people how we would want to be treated in business, a deal can fall through, a customer can become angry, or we can lose our job. This may be the case, but missing out on a deal or being fired after serving someone is much more valuable than closing a deal and keeping a job by taking advantage of someone. As Jonathan Pokluda says, "Obedience is not measured by the outcome."[1]

I have always found it interesting that some people think doing business outside of the values laid out in the Bible will bring more success than following what Scripture teaches. This is simply not the case. Most business books you read today that talk about how to behave in the business-world refer back to a value that is founded in Scripture, whether the author knows it or not. The same goes for all life-hacks, inspirational materials, and motivational books. As Christians, we need not debate the question of "business performance or follow the Bible?" The answer to that question is simply both. By following the teachings of Scripture and being humble, serving others, and putting other's needs before our own, we are living out modern-day best-practices for business and life success. They go hand in hand. Following these practices does not guarantee riches or fame, but it does allow us to be confident in the abilities God has given us to use where He has currently placed us.

This is an incredibly difficult line to walk, but with time, practice, prayer, and consistent time in Scripture, we can gain wisdom and understanding about how best to serve those around us while being confident in our God-given abilities.

Who could be against us? With this Christ-centered confidence in mind as you walk into your office, your conference room, your classroom, your home, or whatever space God has placed you at this point in your life, there is no room for fear. If no one and no thing can prosper against us (Isaiah 54:17), there truly is nothing to worry about. With nothing to worry about, confidence comes naturally. With confidence, we can perform our tasks and duties to our full potential as we pursue excellence. As we become excellent in our God-given abilities, we will gain more influence with those around us. As we gain more influence, we can spread the Good News of the Gospel to those whom we have the ability to influence. There is a beautiful connection between confidence and sharing the Gospel. When the enemy paralyzes us with fear, he breaks down the previously described chain of events so that the Gospel will never be shared and we become ineffective. Remember who is on your side, and you will not fall into the distractionary traps that are crying out for your attention on your pursuit of excellence for influence.

What could be possible in your life if you truly understood that no one and no thing can be against us?

Part Four: The Impact of a Commitment to Excellence

Chapter Ten
Multiplication of Impact

The reason the title "Multiplication of Impact" has been given to this chapter is because I want to discuss what can happen when we have done excellent work and earned influence in our companies, our industries, and in culture. However, before we talk about "what can happen," I want to briefly discuss "what we need to do that we aren't doing now." Sadly, I believe we are not doing the one thing we have been called to do with the influence we have now. If that is the case, then it doesn't matter how much influence we have, we will continue to be ineffective for the Gospel of Jesus Christ.

So, before we talk about what can happen when we do what Jesus has called us to do, we need to take an honest look at ourselves to see if we are living like Jesus has called us to live.

In Matthew 28:18-20, Jesus gives us His final command, The Great Commission, which says: "And Jesus came and said to them, 'All authority in heaven and on earth has been given to me. Go therefore and make disciples of all nations, baptizing them in the name of the Father and of the Son and of the Holy Spirit, teaching them to observe all that I have commanded you. And behold, I am with you always, to the end of the age.'" In that moment, Jesus gave the charge that would be with us "to the end of the age." Notice how Jesus did not say to only share the Gospel with some people, but to <u>all</u> people. We are to grow the Church in all nations, all industries, all professions, all ages, etc. This is our last command and one that is to be followed at all times.

As discussed previously in this book, we spend a huge portion of our lives at our jobs, or at least working to some extent. Sadly, based on an honest audit of our conversations and the way we spend our time, it seems as though many Christians do not think The Great Commission applies when they are working.

Humans are master rationalizers. We will tell ourselves things like, "It's not appropriate to talk about that here," or "I haven't built a relationship with that person well enough yet," or maybe "I'm way too busy to have conversations like this with co-workers," or even "I'll get fired if I talk about that here." These all might seem valid in our minds, but God's logic is almost always outside of our understanding. Imagine for a moment if the disciples had only shared the Gospel when it was safe, convenient, and comfortable. They would have never shared the Gospel with the Romans, they would have been silent while sitting in prison cells, they would have never challenged the leading religious authorities of their day, and their lives honestly would have been comfortable. Maybe they would have tried to simply share the Gospel through how they live their lives, by example.

This "comfortable Christianity" is simply not the Truth, not what Christ has called us to, and not what the Holy Spirit has kept in Scripture for us to model our lives after. In fact, the opposite is actually what we are called to do. In Philippians 1:21, Paul writes, "For me to live is Christ, and to die is gain." Paul is saying that as long as he is alive and here on earth, his only job is to share the Gospel wherever he is and in whatever he is doing.

But maybe we are thinking that "To live is Christ" could mean being silent, or not pushy, about our faith. Scripture would consistently disagree with that idea. In Acts 4, Peter and John were arrested for sharing the Gospel in places where it was not allowed. While standing before the council, Peter and John are told in verse 18 "not to speak or teach at all in the name of Jesus." This is a pretty direct command not to share the Gospel from leaders who seemingly have earthly power over them. We may think, or even know, that we are not to speak or teach of the name of Jesus at our jobs or at our place of residence. The way we have responded to this perceived command throughout our lives might look different from how

Peter and John responded. In verses 19-21, Peter and John responded by saying, "'Whether it is right in the sight of God to listen to you rather than to God, you must judge, for we cannot but speak of what we have seen and heard.' And when they had further threatened them, they let them go, finding no way to punish them, because of the people, for all were praising God for what had happened."

When commanded to no longer speak of Jesus, Peter and John responded from a place of honesty that they simply have to talk about the Truth. Is this what we believe about the Bible, the Gospel, and our Lord? Are we so confident in the Truth laid out in Scripture that we would respond this way when asked not to share the Gospel with others?

Or maybe we would never be asked not to speak of the Gospel with others because we have never shared the Gospel with others to begin with. That could potentially be an even more honest realization for some of us. I pray that if this is you, that you would realize God has called you to a far greater part in His plan and desires for you to share the Truth with those around you, no matter the cost.

I share these verses because I fear that as professing Christians, we have taken a back seat to worldly sets of values and ideas where we think we would rather not step on any toes than share the Gospel and potentially impact someone's eternity. I think we need to be reminded that Jesus lovingly offended the world with Truth. He was tortured, spit on, and crucified. We are called to live like and speak of someone who was so countercultural that He was kicked out of multiple cities and died a criminal's death, all for sharing the Truth His Father entrusted to Him.

A quote that I heard recently from Richard Branson says, "If you want to change the world, draw a circle around yourself and change everything inside of it."[1] If we want to do what Christ has called us to do and truly make an impact in the Kingdom, then we need to start with ourselves. If you feel that this is where you are, and you are not sharing the Gospel out of fear, complacency, a lack of trust, or any number of other reasons, I challenge you to stop reading this book for right now. Ask God to meet you where you are and give you the belief you need to share the Gospel and be bold for His name.

In Mark 9:14-29, Jesus heals a boy with an unclean spirit. When Jesus comes to help the boy, the boy's father says, "But if you can do anything, have compassion on us and help us." Then Jesus responds saying, "If you can! All things are possible for one who believes." The father then responds with one of the most beautifully honest and prayerful statements given in Scripture, "I believe; help my unbelief!"

If you currently possess a belief like the father in Mark 9, then cry out to God like he did as well. Be honest with God. Confess your unbelief and ask Him to meet you where you are. He will be faithful and give you the faith you need to do what He has called you to do. You simply have to ask for the strength from the one who possesses unlimited strength.

Before moving on in this chapter, spend some time with God and work to get your heart right with Him through an honest conversation. I believe this could be the most important thing you could possibly do with your time.

Once you have spent some time with the Lord and postured your heart in a place that believes God is who He says He is, it is time to talk about what God can do through us in our jobs when we multiply our impact. As discussed in Chapter 3, "Examples of Excellence," when we are excellent in our work, many times, influence follows. Now, this influence can oftentimes turn our hearts against the things of God to where we do the opposite of worship God and begin worshipping ourselves as we discussed last chapter. This is something we must always be aware of and be honest with ourselves about. Sometimes, our influence may make us prideful, and that pride can become a blind spot. As we know, the problem with blind spots is that we can't see them, so it may take a group of fellow Believers to continuously audit your life and your heart with you so you can make sure that you are constantly living the life Jesus has called you to live with the servant's heart Christ has called you to live with.

When excellent work is done for a consistent period of time and influence is earned, there is an opportunity to impact those around you. Think for a moment about all of the worst bosses you or others have had. Many were angry, prideful, unforgiving, immoral, underappreciative, and much more. As someone who has earned a position of leadership through excellent work, you can take all of the characteristics of typical leaders in society and turn them upside-down. You can be a leader that is joyful, a peacemaker, humble, grace-filled, loving, empathetic, and above reproof.

There are many studies that have been done in recent years about how leading with a service-minded intent improves company-wide performance, reduces turnover, increases revenue, and much more. In one impressive study titled, "Seven Pillars of Servant Leadership: Practicing the Wisdom of Leading by Serving," by James W. Sipe, it is shown that servant-led companies produce 14% more pre-tax profit on average than S&P 500 companies, and about 7% higher profits than "Good to Great" companies.[2] There is far too much data on this topic to include in this book, but if you would like to see more, I highly recommend looking through some of these studies. Here's a spoiler: they all tell the same story. Servant-leadership works.

Even for those who are not Believers, servant-leadership can help their organizations reach new heights that they may not have ever even imagined. What is truly interesting is that there have been many books written, videos produced, and seminars spoken on how to be a servant leader. These books, videos, and seminars are great, but all they are doing is attempting to catch up to the Truth already laid out in the Bible. Jesus was the author and perfect example of servant leadership. If you want to see proof of this, start by reading John 13:1-17. When we read this story and remember who Jesus is, we are shown the best example of servant leadership ever given.

Through excellent work, we earn influence, with which we are able to display Christ-centered servant leadership to those around us. This will make an impact on profits and turnover yes, but even more so, it will make an impact on the lives and eternities of those at your organization and in your sphere of influence.

When we are pursuing excellence, serving others, and acting like Jesus did to those around us, people are much more open to listen to what God wants to say through us. This is where the multiplication of impact truly comes into play.

When you have earned influence, you have the opportunity to lead others. When you lead others, you have the opportunity to speak into their lives. As mentioned before, when you do this in a Christ-like way, people might even be inclined to listen to what you have to say. When you have the attention of people, what will you say with the influence God has allowed you to have? This goes back to what we spoke of before and why I challenged you to stop reading if your heart was not in the right place with God. If we won't speak about

Jesus and share His Truth in the situations we are currently in where we do not have much influence, we definitely won't share the Truth when we have influence and are speaking to more people.

Whatever influence you have now, whatever opportunities you have now to share the Gospel, do it. Don't wait for the day you have more influence to start sharing the Good News with others. Luke 16:10 says, "One who is faithful in a very little is also faithful in much, and one who is dishonest in a very little is also dishonest in much." More influence will display the status of our heart, not change it.

Once we have earned influence through excellence, we are able to share the Gospel with even more individuals in more places than we could ever imagine. Bob Goff, a very prestigious lawyer who has also funded schools in war-torn Uganda and written incredible Christ-centered books, says it like this, "Having a day job and earning what I needed was a version of fundraising I could understand. Becoming a lawyer had been an ambition of mine when I was in my twenties, and it was something I was able to do well. I decided to let this earlier ambition serve my next ambition. You can do the same."[3] This is the essence of what we are discussing in this book, and especially this chapter. We are to take the gifts God has given us (in Bob's case being an incredible lawyer), do them to the best of our abilities, and use the money and influence that come from excellent work to fund the Kingdom of God through our time, our money, and our actions.

Imagine if someone like Bob Goff was a terrible lawyer, received terrible reviews from clients, was despised by co-workers, and simply did his job poorly. He would not have earned the funds to establish schools in Uganda (his actual passion) or write three best-selling books that God has used to bring countless lives to know Him more or know Him for the first time.

"Multiplication of Impact" does not equate to money or fame. It brings opportunities for us to play larger parts in God's plan that all may know who He is and what He has done for humanity. It is easy to write this down and easy to read. It is much harder to live. When we are excellent and earn influence, a lot of times we start viewing God as the shovel that leads to the treasure and not the treasure itself. This is why we must constantly be in prayer with God, study His Word, and live in a community that keeps us accountable to use the gifts God has given us to make His name known. As evil as we are, we will pervert the things of God and make them about ourselves. Through daily surrender and through carrying our cross with Christ, we can use the daily blessings bestowed on us by God to proclaim the goodness of God to the world wherever we are and in whatever we do.

When we take full advantage of the influence God gives us through being excellent with the gifts God has given us, we can infiltrate every single board-room, every conference, every podcast, every office, every home, every classroom, and every break-room with the Gospel of Jesus. The world needs to hear this message, and God has graciously allowed us to play a part in His Church.

The "Multiplication of Impact" that can occur is disciples being made in every country, every city, every organization, and every family around the world. Let's get excited about the part we get to play and start sharing the Gospel where we are with whatever influence and opportunities God has given us.

Where has God placed you that you can multiply your impact? What does multiplying your impact look like specifically to you and your situation?

Chapter Eleven
Kingdom Growth

We have discussed how to be Biblically excellent, we have discussed what can come from being excellent, and now I would like to talk about what happens when we apply our God-given influence in a Christ-centered way.

Earlier in the book we discussed Tim Tebow as an example of Christian excellence. In 2009, while playing football for the University of Florida, Tebow felt called to write "John 3:16" on his eye black to be seen on national television. Tebow thought that this small decision might impact just one person. However, millions of people tuned into this game because they wanted to see arguably one of the best collegiate athletes of all time play on live television. By the time the game had ended, over 94 million people had Googled "John 3:16."[1]

Think about how many lives may have been changed eternally that night all because one word and two numbers were written on some eye black for a football game. Now, think about what this would have done if millions of people had not tuned in to the game to watch Tebow compete. Would it have still been impactful? I would say, "yes." Isaiah 55:11 tells us that when we share the Word of God, it never returns void. Even if just one person would have seen John 3:16 that night, it would have been a huge success that God would have used. When we share the Gospel, it is not just about the numbers, it is about proclaiming the name of the Lord wherever we are. However, I think it is also important to realize that when we are excellent by using the gifts God has given us, sometimes God will provide us a larger stage than we could ever imagine to proclaim the

Gospel. This football game was Tim Tebow's stage, and John 3:16 was proclaimed to the world that night.

What stage has God given you to proclaim the Word of God? Do you speak with co-workers and clients frequently? Do you have a position of authority in a boardroom meeting? Do you have a large social media following? Do you have children that look up to you as their father or mother? Do you have neighbors who do not know Jesus? Do you ever ride in an Uber with a driver who needs the message of the Gospel? Matt Chandler once said, "You have never met someone who is a mere mortal. Every single person you have ever met has an eternal destination in one place or the other." If we lived with an eternal, Kingdom growth mindset, we would never take a person, or a conversation, for granted.

One temptation we constantly fall into is being ungrateful for the size of the stage God has currently placed us on. Maybe we wish we were preaching to thousands like Billy Graham every night, but we are actually doing devotions with our five-year-old who can't seem to keep their crayons out of their nose. Or maybe we wish we were the CEO of an organization so we would have more influence over corporate values and mission, but we feel we are stuck filing papers and only speaking with a few co-workers each day. However, let's remember Luke 16:10 again, "One who is faithful in a very little is also faithful in much, and one who is dishonest in a very little is also dishonest in much." If we are not being faithful to proclaim the Gospel where Christ has currently called us and placed us, why then should God allow us to have a larger stage to make His name known?

The truth is, God knows our hearts, and if we have a deep need for our name to be made known and not God's, God knows that. 1 Samuel 16:7 says, "But the Lord said to Samuel, 'Do not look on his appearance or on the height of his stature, because I have rejected him. For the Lord sees not as man sees: man looks on the outward appearance, but the Lord looks on the heart.'" No matter what we do and what the outside world thinks about what we do, God knows our hearts. When our hearts are humbled and are in a place ready to be of service to the plan and will of God, then God will use us more.

To put this into perspective, let's visualize a children's musical. We have all probably been to one or at least seen one in a movie.

The kids are up on stage doing their best to simply remember the words to songs, remember the little hand motions, and not wander off the stage. The people who are enjoying the musical are not enjoying the music, they are enjoying the cuteness of the kids performing. Everyone has their phones out smiling and laughing while the kids are doing their absolute best. If we were honest, their best is not great from a musical perspective. If we had to choose whether we would listen to a Broadway musical or the children's musical, and we were sane, we would choose Broadway ten times out of ten unless our own child was performing in the musical.

Now, imagine with me that the little kids performing took the applause and smiles as a compliment on their actual musical capabilities and decided they were taking the show to Broadway. (This analogy is a stretch but just stick with me here). The kids get to Broadway, they get a massive stage, the perfect time slot on a Friday night, and the show sells out for $1,000 per ticket. In this analogy the only marketing that has been seen about this musical is that it is the new, big show. It is a must-see event.

An hour before the show, the line forms and people are dressed in their nicest suits and dresses ready to witness this majestic new musical. The crowd files into their seats ready for their ears to be graced with voices that contain the quality of Idina Menzel, Lin-Manuel Miranda, and countless other Broadway superstars. The lights dim. The show is about to start.

The curtain comes up and standing before the crowd is a group of five-year-olds in their school clothes trying to sing *Mary Had a Little Lamb*. Emphasis on the word "trying." Little Susie and little Billy can't stop hitting each other. Tommy is digging for gold in his nose. Kate is simply facing the wrong direction. Oh, what is that? Sadly, Mikey decided to walk off stage because he was bored.

The crowd is shocked, stunned, and frankly disappointed. They were cheated. These kids are cute and trying their best, but they are not Broadway ready. The crowd gets up and leaves and the kids feel as though they aren't good musicians anymore.

Who wins in this situation? No one. The children feel sad, the patrons are out of thousands of dollars, and the theater wasted a night when they could have had someone else perform.

Why did I take up so much time with this ridiculous analogy you might ask? Because this is what we do as Christians all the time.

We are sometimes baby Christians. We are just truly getting into the Word of God, just starting our relationship with Him, just beginning to share the Gospel at work, just beginning to venture out of our insecurities and fear in sharing the Gospel with strangers, and we expect God to put us on the biggest stage at the biggest moment.

The same can also be said about things that aren't spiritual. It is no secret that a huge portion of society feels entitled to a promotion, a raise, a bonus, more followers, more likes, etc., when we haven't earned it yet. As Jonathan Pokluda said, "Entitlement is the highest platform from which we fall." We believe we are entitled to a bigger stage. We believe God is holding out on us, so we complain about wanting a bigger stage while standing on the stage God has placed us. While we are complaining, God is asking us to be faithful with where we are and proclaim His name there. God does not promise a larger stage, but He promises more of Himself when we proclaim His name, and shouldn't that be enough?

Since when did the stage God has placed us become a competition? Remember, we are dealing with eternity here. We are not "trying to make a sale." We are sharing the Good News that Jesus came to earth and died for our sins and was raised again three days later. No matter where we are, what we are doing, or if we are in our dream job or not, we declare the Gospel to those around us.

As of the most recent number recorded, there are currently around 7.594 billion people in the world.[2] That means there are 7.594 billion stages that are or are not being used that God has prepared for us while we are living here on earth. Little do we know that there might be a stage that is currently empty because the "performer" might be sitting in the audience of our stage. Once we proclaim the Gospel to them, they will go to their stage and proclaim the name of Jesus as well to a new audience we may never have been able to reach. This is the beautiful cycle that God has called us to participate in.

If we want to truly grow the Kingdom of God, then we need to be thankful for the stage where God has placed us and make the most of it. God might call you to a bigger stage, and he might keep you on your current stage for a long time. It is all part of His perfect plan.

If we think back to the analogy about the little Broadway "stars" that I shared earlier, there is another idea that can be taken away from it as well. Imagine if a theater critic had gone to see the kids perform at their school and found out they were going to perform on Broadway. What would he say? Probably something about how there is no way these kids should be performing, they have no business being on Broadway, and they could learn a thing or two from other theater experts.

This is where being excellent comes in! When we are young (age or experience) in our career journey, young in wisdom, young in influence, etc., it is the perfect time to learn as much as possible from those who are much farther along than us who have been Biblically excellent for a long time and have used their influence to grow the Kingdom of God. As we perform the best we possibly can at our jobs, in our marriages, in our service, in whatever we do, we are also learning more and being given more influence. We are called to start influencing the world for the Gospel where we already are instead of waiting until we are given a larger stage.

We must be faithful where and how often we proclaim the Gospel, grow in excellence, and trust that God will continue to guide us towards those who need to hear the Good News of Jesus. This is how Kingdom Growth happens.

1 Corinthians 12:12 says, "For just as the body is one and has many members, and all the members of the body, though many, are one body, so it is with Christ." The Church is a team full of millions of people all playing their part and proclaiming the Gospel on the stage that God has placed them. Some parts seem bigger than others, some stages seem larger, but to God they are equally important.

How tragic would it be to go through life sitting on our stage complaining about how we wish God had called us to a bigger stage when God had one prepared for us if we had only used the gifts He had given us to glorify Him more. Let's decide that today is the day we use our gifts, become excellent at what we do, gain influence, and share the Gospel through word and deed throughout the entire journey.

The last "stage" analogy I will use in this chapter is this: Imagine you had one show a night for a year. Each stage and theater were bigger each night as the year went on. Imagine if for the first 364 performances all you did was walk out on the stage and talk about how incredible your 365th performance was going to be. Imagine how many missed opportunities you would have to perform, how bad your reviews would be, and how terrible your skills would be by the time you arrived at the 365th performance compared to if you had performed your best for the previous 364 days.

The only sure thing in life is that change is coming. When we are excellent, new stages will constantly come our way. Don't wait for the final stage to start proclaiming the Gospel. Don't waste the influence God has already given you for the influence you think God will give you later. The souls you have the opportunity to share Christ with right now are just as valued by God as the souls you will talk to later. And if we are honest, we will be much better and much more confident at sharing the Gospel later in life if we start now. We also may not even get a "tomorrow." Proverbs 27:1 says, "Do not boast about tomorrow, for you do not know what a day may bring."

Don't waste your current influence. Don't neglect your God-given stage. God has you where you are to grow His Kingdom. If you don't share the Good News, your "audience" might tune into a different stage that is proclaiming something else besides Christ. Don't lose sight of the fact that every day you are entering a battle to point people to Jesus and away from the world. The world will not stop crying out for the eternal attention of those around you, and neither should you. The difference is your message of Good News points to life, and the world's message points to death.

If you truly love others, you simply cannot stop from sharing the Gospel with them. There is too much at stake. Trust God's promises and be faithful where you have been placed now. Why should God allow you to have more influence when you are neglecting the opportunities He has already placed in front of you? You can do it. God is with you, and He is faithful every time.

What are the current stages God has placed in your life for you to proclaim the Gospel through words and actions?

Chapter Twelve

What if?

As we conclude this book, I want to end with a question: What would happen if the Church pursued excellence, gained influence, and shared the Gospel at all stages of the process? What if?

As I have stated previously, we are not being excellent for our own glory. The reason we are striving for excellence is because that is what God expects of us. When we are excellent, opportunities are made available to speak with new people, know more people, and impact more people in an eternal way. Biblical excellence may not equate to a promotion or a raise every single time, but if we are faithful to serve Jesus and be excellent and faithful where He has currently placed us, He will give us more opportunities to serve Him. The influence we are looking for has nothing to do with money or fame. Sometimes money and fame come from being excellent, and if that is the case, then praise God for that. But the influence we desire is the opportunity to share the Gospel with more people. Being excellent in our work, in our marriages, in our relationships, in our schooling, in our hobbies, and every other area of life will give us those opportunities. When we do everything with the qualities of Christ, like being ethical, forgiving, hard-working, and more, people will notice that we are different and want to know what makes us different. That is where we get to share the story, grace, and love of Christ.

What would the world look like with Christian leadership in every industry, every family, every school, every government agency, and every other organization? You may think I am being naive, but I choose to believe that Ephesians 3:20-21 is true. It says, "Now to him who is able to do far more abundantly than all that we ask or think, according to the power at work within us, to him be glory in the church and in Christ Jesus throughout all generations, forever and ever. Amen." Amen is right!

If we believe that the Bible is true, that Jesus is Lord, that He loves us, and that He wants to use us to fulfill His plan, then this verse should be our battle cry as we enter into the workforce each day. We should feel like William Wallace in *Braveheart* crying out for freedom when we wake up each morning! God is able to do far more abundantly than all we could ever ask or even think. So, let's not put God in a box. Let's dream big!

Now, let's envision this again: What would the world look like with Christian leadership? Scripture tells us that these leaders would fear God, be trustworthy, hate dishonest gain, seek God's counsel, delight in the Lord, find stability, protect themselves from corruption, be rooted in righteousness, and much more (Exodus 18:21, Psalm 32:8, Psalm 37:3-4, Psalm 37:7, Psalm 78:72, Proverbs 4:23, Proverbs 16:12). If every

CEO, principal, parent, politician, and worker possessed all of the qualities listed above, the world would look much different.

With Christian leaders impacting their growing spheres of influence for Jesus and making the Gospel known there, we would see church attendance sky-rocket instead of drop by 20% like it has over the past 20 years.[1] The 153 million orphans in the world would be cared for intensely and lovingly by people who see them like Jesus sees them.[2] The 150 million homeless people in the world would have shelter provided by giving, open hands.[3] Toxic work cultures would be a thing of the past. There are countless other positive outcomes that could occur through Christians becoming excellent in the areas they are called. Offices, organizations, lives, cities, countries, and the world would be changed.

I believe it is also vital to point out that no matter how excellent you are, how hard you are pursuing Jesus, and how much you are proclaiming the Gospel, we are still human and are still going to make many mistakes. If the leaders around the world professed Jesus over fame and fortune would things be different? Yes, absolutely. Would there still be many issues because we are still evil sinners who need daily grace? Yes, absolutely. The difference would be that leaders who pursue Jesus would let go of their pride and confess their mistakes. Leaders would hold each other accountable to what Scripture outlines as necessary, upright, and true. Mistakes would happen, but so would repentance. This is another effect of Christian leadership.

If Christians were known as hard workers, were excellent at what they do, and possessed the characteristics of Jesus in the process, ultimately, we would be able to sow more seeds for God to use to grow His eternal Kingdom. As we discussed early in this book, no one wants to hear from the salesperson at the bottom of the sales board. No one wants advice from the teacher who complains about their students all the time. No one wants to live like the CEO who berates their employees and never shows empathy. When we work poorly, we represent God poorly.

Titus 3:1-11 speaks about this:

Remind them to be submissive to rulers and authorities, to be obedient, to be ready for every good work, to speak evil of no one, to avoid quarreling, to be gentle, and to show perfect courtesy toward all people. For we ourselves were once foolish, disobedient, led astray, slaves to various passions and pleasures, passing our days in malice and envy, hated by others and hating one another. But when the goodness and loving kindness of God our Savior appeared, he saved us, not because of works done by us in righteousness, but according to his own mercy, by the washing of regeneration and renewal of the Holy Spirit, whom he poured out on us richly through Jesus Christ our Savior, so that being justified by his grace we might become heirs according to the hope of eternal life. The saying is trustworthy, and I want you to insist on these things, so that those who have believed in God may be careful to devote themselves to good works. These things are excellent and profitable for people. But avoid foolish controversies, genealogies, dissensions, and quarrels about the law, for they are unprofitable and worthless. As for a person who stirs up division, after warning him once and then twice, have nothing more to do with him, knowing that such a person is warped and sinful; he is self-condemned.

In this passage of Scripture, we are shown how to live, how to speak, what happens when we follow these instructions, and what happens when we don't. I am thankful we serve a God so wise and caring that He would outline something this clearly for us. If you remember one thing from this book, remember to cling to and meditate on Titus 3:1-11. It is a perfect outline for excellence in the Body of Christ.

When we are excellent in what we do, people will take notice. That is where influence comes in. If we are not careful, we will think that this is an opportunity to take any sort of credit for what we do and the excellence we have achieved. But notice what the previous passage says, "He saved us, not because of works done by us in righteousness, but according to his own mercy, by the washing of regeneration and renewal of the Holy Spirit." We did not save ourselves. We did not achieve excellence ourselves. Solely because of the goodness and grace of God are we able to have gifts, use them well, and gain influence. What do we do with that influence? We point others to Christ. It is never about us. Galatians 6:14 says, "But far be it from me to boast except in the cross of our Lord Jesus Christ, by which the world has been crucified to me, and I to the world." When we are excellent and have opportunities to boast, we boast only in the Lord. Verbally, we turn all praise into worship of God and His grace. With our actions, we serve excellently and intentionally. We are crucified to Christ, and we are to serve others and point others to Christ who was crucified for us.

In Acts 10, Peter is brought before Cornelius, a centurion. Cornelius, upon seeing Peter, immediately falls down and worships Peter. Most of us would probably let the centurion worship us for a little while. Peter on the other hand does the opposite. In Acts 10:26, Peter lifts up the Centurion and says, "Stand up; I too am a man." Peter then turns the conversation to things of eternal value and focuses on God.

How does this Bible passage apply to us today? Maybe you win an award, set a new sales record, get a promotion, start a new company, graduate at the top of your class, have a successful IPO, or have countless other achievements. What do we do when the spotlight shines on us? The character and Christ-likeness of a person shines brightest or fades darkest when the spotlight shines on them. If we are excellent and given influence, these spotlight moments are when the Gospel must be proclaimed without apology. This is the simplest challenge of this book but also the hardest. We all want to work harder, be excellent, and earn influence, but we really like getting the credit for things. I mean, we earned it right?

Hebrews 3:4 says, "For every house is built by someone, but the builder of all things is God." We may have built the house with the tools God gave us. We may put blood, sweat, and tears into the excellent work we do. But God is the original builder of all things. God is the builder of our gifts and our talents. God gave us the ability to be excellent. Why should we take any credit for something that we had nothing to do with? When the spotlight is on us, it is time to give all praise back to God, share the Gospel with others, and make known the name of Jesus.

I heard a story recently about someone who had shared the Gospel with over 250 people in a city that might be considered the "Buckle of the Bible Belt." Everyone assumes everyone else is a Christian. Everyone assumes everyone else goes to church. Many don't share the Gospel intentionally because why should you if everyone knows Jesus, right? Well, this individual decided he would share the Gospel anyway because Isaiah 55:11 tells us the Word of God never returns void.

When he told me that he had shared the Gospel with over 250 people, he asked me how many did I think actually had a relationship with Jesus out of the people he spoke with. I wanted to be safe so I didn't underestimate it too much, so I guessed half. 125 people out of 250. His response shocked me. The actual answer? Four. Four people out of 250 knew

Jesus Christ as Lord and Savior in the Buckle of the Bible Belt. If we believe that the Bible is true and that an eternity away from Jesus is what we are destined for if we don't know Him, then that means out of 250 people in the Bible Belt, only four were going to spend an eternity with Jesus. If we turn his ratio of four out of 250 into a percentage, then the percentage of people who knew Jesus would be about 1.6%. This broke my heart. How many years have I (and so many others) gone through life, jobs, restaurants, grocery stores, gyms, etc., not sharing the Gospel because of an assumption with absolutely no backing?

I decided I would test out his numbers for myself. I decided I would start sharing the Gospel with anyone I could (you know, what the Bible calls us to do). After a few weeks of doing this, I can honestly say his numbers were wrong. My numbers turned out to be a whopping 0% who knew Jesus. You might be thinking I am being too judgmental and it is not my place to decide if someone knows Jesus or not. I agree with you, that is not my place. However, when you ask if they have a faith or a belief in God and every single person says, "No," I think it is safe to say I can chalk that up to a no.

Why do I share these alarming numbers? I share these numbers because there are people in our offices, in boardrooms around the world, in classrooms, in government buildings, and in homes that have never put their faith in Jesus. There are people we will see every day for years of our lives whose souls could be crying out in despair. People we share space with could be looking to fill the God-shaped vacuum in their souls with countless other ultimately empty solutions. Maybe all they need is one person to share the Gospel with them. Maybe God is asking that you be that person. Actually, I don't think it is a maybe. If there is someone that doesn't know Jesus, we are absolutely called to go and make disciples, baptizing them in the name of the Father, of the Son, and of the Holy Spirit (Matthew 28:16-20).

As we pursue excellence, we will cross paths with countless individuals with whom we may have some sort of influence. Will we use that influence for an eternal purpose or a comfortable one? As we are faithful in being excellent where God has placed us, and sharing the Gospel there, God will give us more and more opportunities to proclaim the Good News to more people, we just have to look for and ask for those opportunities.

It is said that there are three types of motivation: Fear, Incentive, and Attitude. We know fear and incentive don't work. If you don't believe me, there are many other better-written books that can attest to that. However, attitude works incredibly well. Why? Because the people being motivated believe that what they are doing is right and beneficial. Quite simply, they buy-in to the message on their own and aren't forced. This can be applied to our Christian walk as well.

As we are excellent and gain influence, and maybe even possess leadership positions, we have the opportunity to help change the attitudes towards the Gospel of Jesus Christ. We don't have to be the fear-based Bible-bashing people on street corners yelling at people to repent or go to hell. We don't have to be the incentive-based people who just talk about how good heaven will be. Through portraying the characteristics and the attitude of Jesus, others will want to know more, and their attitudes will change towards God and towards Christianity. When they want to know more, we have the opportunity to play a part in God's eternal plan and share the Gospel with them. Once we share the Gospel with them, we may even have the opportunity to disciple or mentor them in the faith as they wrestle with questions and verses as a new Believer. We get to partner with God in the most important job of all time. There is no greater joy than this.

When the leaders of the world are being led by the Creator of the world, the God-glorifying purpose of humanity and the beauty of the Gospel outshines all darkness.

Who are some people in your life or some places you go to that you can share the Gospel of Jesus with today? This week? This month? This year?

Conclusion

2 Corinthians 3:18 says, "And we all, with unveiled face, beholding the glory of the Lord, are being transformed into the same image from one degree of glory to another. For this comes from the Lord who is the Spirit." Living out the Gospel in our lives and in our careers is a lifelong process. There will be valleys and there will be mountains. If you have accepted the challenge to be Biblically excellent and faithful in all that you do and to point to the message of the Gospel with every ounce of influence you have, then your life is about to start looking a lot different.

When you are saved, nothing can snatch you out of God's eternal grasp (John 10:28), so what is the best that the Enemy can do? As we discussed previously, he can make you ineffective, ruin your witness, and steal you away from your community to make you feel alone.

If you are a lukewarm Christian, if that even is possible, then the enemy simply is not worried about you. You are not doing anything to move forward the message of the Gospel and push back darkness anyways, so why should he dedicate any time or energy towards you? However, if you have accepted this challenge and are making the Gospel message known in all areas of your life, you will begin to face more temptation, more trials, and more difficulties than you have ever experienced. The reason? Satan is terrified of what the Holy Spirit is going to do through you.

I don't say this to scare you. I say this to prepare you. The Bible tells us to flee temptation (Matthew 26:41), and I believe that fleeing starts way before the temptation actually begins. If we know that the enemy's mission is always to steal, kill, and destroy (John 10:10), then we need to be prepared.

Now that you have been warned about the temptations and trials that are coming, I want to encourage you to do a few things:

1. Become Biblically literate. The biggest problem today is that we simply do not know the Bible. If we do not hide God's Word in our hearts, then what will stand

against the conflicting messages of the enemy when they come our way? Start reading the words of our Creator every single day. Do not become a slave to what sounds right, become a student of Truth given to us by the Creator of all things.

2. Get to know the God you are serving. Spending time in prayer is something that we should do without ceasing (1 Thessalonians 5:17). The fact is you and I are not strong enough to resist temptation, flee from the enemy, be excellent in our careers, and use our influence to share the Gospel every single day. No matter how much positive self-talk we have, how many good books we read, inspirational videos we watch, and self-love we practice, we will always fail at combating the enemy without the help of our Savior and Conqueror. It is vital that we ask God for strength, wisdom, patience, guidance, purity, and much more every single day. We need to truly know Him and love Him. We can't do that if we don't have consistent communication with Him. Let's pray more.

3. Find and build a Christian community. The third and final tip I want to give here is to make every effort to surround yourself with others who love the Lord and who are pursuing Him. Can't find one? Create one. Start a local chapter of Christian professionals, create a group text with friends where you share Scriptures and prayer requests. Get creative! Also, make sure that you join a local, Bible-believing church and get involved. Join a small group there, serve the Body of Christ there, give of your time and your money there. It is worth it, I promise. If you are having a hard time with this aspect of it, see my contact information at the back of this book. Send me an email or contact me on social media and I will do everything I possibly can to help you find a local church that you can join and a body of Believers that you can get to know.

Be ready for trials that are coming. It is not a matter of if they will come, but when they will come. It saddens me to think about how many Christian leaders have fallen away from the faith and haven't finished the race because they were not ready for the trials and challenges coming their way. Please don't be one of those people. Become Biblically literate so you can decipher what is of God and what is not. Pray without ceasing so that your personal relationship with the Lord grows. Find and build a strong Christian community that can pick you up and encourage you. There will be hills, there will be valleys, and in both, God is still good and we are still to be faithful to the calling that He has placed on our lives.

One of the most beautiful lyrics of our time comes from the song "Highlands (Song of Ascent)," written by Benjamin Hastings and Joel Houston. The lyrics say this:

> I will praise You on the mountain
> And I will praise You when the mountain's in my way
> You're the summit where my feet are
> So, I will praise You in the valleys all the same
> No less God within the shadows
> No less faithful when the night leads me astray
> You're the heaven where my heart is
> In the highlands and the heartache all the same

> Whatever I walk through
>
> Wherever I am
>
> Your Name can move mountains
>
> Wherever I stand.
>
> And if ever I walk through
>
> The valley of death
>
> I'll sing through the shadows
>
> My song of ascent

Through the valleys and on the mountaintops, in persecution and in the mundane, God is faithful to us. Let's be faithful to Him.

As we wrap up our time together in this book, I want to leave you with this verse: Matthew 9:37, "Then he said to his disciples, 'The harvest is plentiful, but the laborers are few.'"

In the last chapter I shared some alarming numbers about how few individuals had a relationship with Jesus from the small sample size I have had experience with recently. There was one number I failed to share, though. 99.3%. This number equates to the amount of people that were open to speaking about Jesus, their faith or lack of faith, religion, and the Gospel message. People don't know Jesus and are willing to talk about Him. The harvest is indeed plentiful and the laborers are tragically few. If you are like me, sometimes you might fall into the trap of thinking you are a laborer, but in reality, you are only part-time. Only on Sundays after a good sermon, only after that one song comes on in the car with the powerful chorus, only when God hands us opportunities on a silver platter. Let's become full-time laborers that harvest even when it is uncomfortable and even painful. The Word of God will not return void. As Os Guinness once said, "We can turn an ordinary job into an extraordinary mission if we realize that God has placed us in our work as an opportunity to influence others for His Kingdom."[1]

I am writing this conclusion during the Covid-19 pandemic. The world is shaken, people are scared, companies are being turned upside-down, and the harvest is plentiful. This verse has never been truer in my lifetime than it is at this very moment. I have a feeling it will only be truer as the days go on.

In tragedy, God sparks change in the hearts of His people. The moment in which we are currently living and the moment you are currently reading this is a season of harvesting. Hearts are ready to hear from the Lord and cling to His Truth. The world is ready to proclaim the name of Jesus as Lord. However, there is a problem.

The last five words of that verse read, "but the laborers are few." During this time of uncertainty and fear, the world needs Christians to rise up and become laborers in the harvest. Make the decision that you are going to be a full-time laborer with Jesus in every area of your life. Don't limit God to Sundays or simply not the 1,800 hours you are working this year. The Body of Christ needs to become full-time laborers. The Church needs to be the Church in our offices, in our classrooms, and in our homes. The world is waiting.

Will you pursue excellence in everything you do, in every place you have been called, and use the influence you gain to proclaim the only name that is worthy to be praised? God is ready to move. Let's do this together Church.

Contact Information

I truly hope and pray that God spoke to you through this book. There is nothing that would mean more to me than to hear from you. Please reach out to me at the contact information below to share anything that God taught you, any updates on how sharing the Gospel in your workplace has gone, any celebratory messages about individuals giving their lives to Christ, with any questions you may have, any prayer requests you may have, or simply to talk. As mentioned previously in the book, if you are looking for a body of Believers to meet with in your area, please let me know. I will do anything I can to help you get plugged in to a local Church. Thank you for reading, and I look forward to hearing from you.

Email: jonaherbe@gmail.com

Instagram: @jonaherbe

Twitter: @jonaherbe

Sources by Chapter

Introduction:

1. Bayers, Chip. "The Inner Bezos." *Wired*, Conde Nast, www.wired.com/1999/03/bezos-3/.
2. Ponciano, Jonathan. *Jeff Bezos Becomes The First Person Ever Worth $200 Billion*. 27 Aug. 2020, www.forbes.com/sites/jonathanponciano/2020/08/26/worlds-richest-billionaire-jeff-bezos-first-200-billion/?sh=dabadcb4db7b.
3. Palmer, A. (2020, August 26). Jeff Bezos is now worth more than $200 billion. Retrieved November 17, 2020, from https://www.cnbc.com/2020/08/26/amazon-ceo-jeff-bezos-worth-more-than-200-billion.html
4. McLellan, E. (2019). *Favor Follows Hustle*. Speech presented at Shoreline City Church.
5. Edwards, R. (2020, October 27). Crime and the Coronavirus: What You Need to Know. Retrieved 2020, from https://www.safewise.com/blog/covid-19-crimes/#:~:text=Car%20thefts%20and%20break%2Dins,stolen%20so%20far%20in%202020.

Chapter One:

1. Carr, S. (2020, November 07). How Many Ads Do We See A Day? 2020 Daily Ad Exposure Revealed! Retrieved

November 23, 2020, from https://ppcprotect.com/how-many-ads-do-we-see-a-day/

2. Mammoser, G. (2018, December 10). Social Media Increases Depression and Loneliness. Retrieved November 23, 2020, from https://www.healthline.com/health-news/social-media-use-increases-depression-and-loneliness

3. Jobs, S. (2005, June 12). *Stanford Commencement Speech*. Speech presented at Stanford Commencement.

Chapter Two:

1. Clifton, J. (2020, January 13). The World's Broken Workplace. Retrieved November 23, 2020, from https://news.gallup.com/opinion/chairman/212045/world-broken-workplace.aspx

2. Thompson, K. (2018, March 11). What Percentage of Your Life Will You Spend at Work? Retrieved November 23, 2020, from https://revisesociology.com/2016/08/16/percentage-life-work/

3. Bodnick, M. (2013, March 27). Why Do So Many People Hate Their Jobs? Retrieved November 23, 2020, from

https://www.forbes.com/sites/quora/2013/03/27/why-do-so-many-people-hate-their-jobs/?sh=7dbd04545b6a

4. Lewis, C. S. (2013). *A year with C.S. Lewis: 365 daily readings from his classic works*. London, UK: William Collins.

Chapter Three:

1. *Entreleadership: How to Run a Be-Rich Business with David Salyers* [Radio broadcast]. (2019, August 5). In *Entreleadership Podcast*.

2. Giving Back. Retrieved November 23, 2020, from https://www.chick-fil-a.com/about/giving-back

3. Who We Are. Retrieved November 23, 2020, from https://www.chick-fil-a.com/about/who-we-are

4. Kelso, A. (2019, June 25). Chick-fil-A Named America's Favorite Restaurant Chain - Again. Retrieved November 23, 2020, from https://www.forbes.com/sites/aliciakelso/2019/06/25/chick-fil-a-named-americas-favorite-restaurant-chain--again/?sh=2bac0d084c91

5. Smith, J. (2017, November 19). 'Lightning in a bottle': Local impact of Magnolia could long outlive 'Fixer Upper'.

Retrieved November 23, 2020, from https://wacotrib.com/news/business/lightning-in-a-bottle-local-impact-of-magnolia-could-long/article_ac5ce49b-9a2b-568f-a3e6-ff8d31580a5f.html

6. TripAdvisor. (2018, January 09). TripAdvisor Announces Travelers' Choice Destinations On The Rise Awards Revealing Top Trending Travel Spots For 2018. Retrieved November 23, 2020, from https://ir.tripadvisor.com/news-releases/news-release-details/tripadvisor-announces-travelers-choice-destinations-rise-awards

7. Darwish, M. (2020, August 05). Chip & Joanna Gaines Reviving 'Fixer Upper' for Magnolia Network. Retrieved November 23, 2020, from https://www.tvinsider.com/944158/fixer-upper-revival-reboot-chip-joanna-gaines-magnolia-network/

8. Gaines, J. (2020, May 26). Chip and Joanna Gaines: White Chair Film. Retrieved November 23, 2020, from https://www.iamsecond.com/film/chip-and-joanna-gaines/

9. Strain, L. S., & Hudson, G. W. (1986). *The story of Paul J. Meyer: The million dollar personal success plan*. Hollywood, FL: F. Fell.
10. Welcome Letter. Retrieved November 23, 2020, from https://www.lmi-world.com/who-we-are/welcome-letter/
11. Christian Stewardship. Retrieved November 23, 2020, from https://pauljmeyer.com/the-legacy/christian-stewardship/
12. Dirocco, M. (2018, April 23). Tim Tebow: Swamp King. Retrieved November 23, 2020, from https://www.mensjournal.com/sports/tim-tebow-swamp-king/
13. Tebow, T. (2008, September 27). [Interview]. ESPN.
14. Staff, S. (2012, August 29). Hardest Working Players: NFL. Retrieved November 23, 2020, from https://www.si.com/nfl/2012/08/29/29hardest-working-players-nfl
15. Tebow, T., & Gregory, A. J. (2016). *Shaken: Discovering your true identity in the midst of life's storms*. New York, NY: Waterbrook.

16. ECPA. (2017). ECPA Announces the Winners of the 2017 Christian Book Awards®. Retrieved from https://www.ecpa.org/news/343436/ECPA-Announces-the-Winners-of-the-2017-Christian-Book-Awards.htm

Chapter Four

1. Sinek, S. (2019). *Start with why: How great leaders inspire everyone to take action*. London: Portfolio Penguin.

Chapter Five

1. Backman, M. (2017, December 17). Here's How Many Hours the Average American Works Per Year. Retrieved November 30, 2020, from https://www.fool.com/careers/2017/12/17/heres-how-many-hours-the-average-american-works-pe.aspx

2. Ziglar, Z. (2004). *Zig: The autobiography of Zig Ziglar*. New York, NY: Doubleday.

Chapter Six

1. Maxwell, J. C. (2017). *The power of significance: How purpose changes your life*. New York, NY: Center Street.

Chapter Seven

1. Bloom, J. (2020, December 09). Lay Aside the Weight of Perfection. Retrieved December 09, 2020, from https://www.desiringgod.org/articles/lay-aside-the-weight-of-perfection
2. Gallagher, W. (2020, March). How Apple owes everything to its 1977 Apple II computer. Retrieved December 09, 2020, from https://appleinsider.com/articles/20/04/18/how-apple-owes-everything-to-its-1977-apple-ii-computer
3. Apple III Chaos: Apple's First Failure. (2016, June 24). Retrieved December 09, 2020, from https://lowendmac.com/2015/apple-iii-chaos-apples-first-failure/
4. Taube, A. (2014, January 22). How The Greatest Super Bowl Ad Ever - Apple's '1984' - Almost Didn't Make It To Air. Retrieved December 09, 2020, from https://www.businessinsider.com/apple-super-bowl-retrospective-2014-1

Chapter Eight

1. Blount, N. (2017). *Game Changer: A Playbook for Winning at Life*. Travelers Rest, SC: True Potential.

2. Clear, J. (2020, November 11). Motivation: The Scientific Guide on How to Get and Stay Motivated. Retrieved December 09, 2020, from https://jamesclear.com/motivation

Chapter Nine

1. Pokluda, J. (2016, November 13). *Extraordinary Living Marked by Ordinary Obedience*. Lecture presented in Watermark Community Church, Dallas.

Chapter Ten

1. Mejia, Z. (2018, October 25). Billionaire Richard Branson says this visual trick will help you reach your biggest goals. Retrieved December 09, 2020, from https://www.cnbc.com/2017/11/24/billionaire-richard-branson-says-this-visual-trick-will-help-you-reach-your-biggest-goals.html
2. Sipe, J. W., & Frick, D. M. (2015). *Seven pillars of servant leadership: Practicing the wisdom of leading by serving*. Mahwah: Paulist.
3. Goff, B. (2020). *Dream big: Know what you want, why you want it, and what you're going to do about it*. Nashville, TN: Nelson Books, an imprint of Thomas Nelson.

Chapter Eleven

1. Thomasos, C. (2016, April 05). Tim Tebow: Don't Underestimate God, Who Used My John 3:16 Eye Black to Reach 94 Million People. Retrieved December 10, 2020, from https://www.christianpost.com/news/tim-tebow-god-john-316-bible-verse-eye-black-role-model.html

2. Current World Population. (n.d.). Retrieved December 10, 2020, from https://www.worldometers.info/world-population/

Chapter Twelve

1. Jones, J. (2020, November 23). U.S. Church Membership Down Sharply in Past Two Decades. Retrieved December 10, 2020, from https://news.gallup.com/poll/248837/church-membership-down-sharply-past-two-decades.aspx

2. How Many Orphans Worldwide? What to Do? (n.d.). Retrieved December 10, 2020, from https://adoption.org/many-orphans-worldwide

3. Chamie, J. (2017, July 13). As Cities Grow, So Do the Numbers of Homeless. Retrieved December 10, 2020,

from https://yaleglobal.yale.edu/content/cities-grow-so-do-numbers-homeless

Conclusion

1. Guinness, O. (2018). *The call: Finding and fulfilling God's purpose for your life*. Nashville, TN: W Publishing Group, an imprint of Thomas Nelson.